M000308127

Libraries, Human Rights, and Social Justice

Libraries, Human Rights, and Social Justice

Enabling Access and Promoting Inclusion

Paul T. Jaeger
Natalie Greene Taylor
Ursula Gorham

ROWMAN & LITTLEFIELD
Lanham • Boulder • New York • London

Published by Rowman & Littlefield
A wholly owned subsidiary of The Rowman & Littlefield Publishing Group, Inc.
4501 Forbes Boulevard, Suite 200, Lanham, Maryland 20706
www.rowman.com

Unit A, Whitacre Mews, 26-34 Stannary Street, London SE11 4AB

Copyright © 2015 by Rowman & Littlefield

All rights reserved. No part of this book may be reproduced in any form or by any electronic or mechanical means, including information storage and retrieval systems, without written permission from the publisher, except by a reviewer who may quote passages in a review.

British Library Cataloguing in Publication Information Available

Library of Congress Cataloging-in-Publication Data

Jaeger, Paul T., 1974–
Libraries, human rights, and social justice : enabling access and promoting inclusion / Paul T. Jaeger, Natalie Greene Taylor, Ursula Gorham.
p. cm.
Includes bibliographical references and index.
ISBN 978-1-4422-5051-2 (cloth : alk. paper) – ISBN 978-1-4422-5052-9 (ebook)
1. Libraries and society. 2. Library science–Social aspects. 3. Library science–Political aspects. 4. Technological literacy. 5. Information policy. 6. Digital divide. 7. Human rights. 8. Social justice. I. Taylor, Natalie Greene, 1987– II. Gorham, Ursula, 1975– III. Title.
Z716.4.J34 2015
021.2–dc23
2015005160

∞ ™ The paper used in this publication meets the minimum requirements of American National Standard for Information Sciences Permanence of Paper for Printed Library Materials, ANSI/NISO Z39.48-1992.

Printed in the United States of America

Contents

List of Abbreviations

AALL	American Association of Law Librarians
AASL	American Association of School Librarians
ACA	Affordable Care Act
ACRL	Association of College and Research Libraries
ALA	The American Library Association
ALISE	Association of Library and Information Science Educators
ARL	Association of Research Libraries
ARRA	American Reinvestment and Recovery Act
BIP	Broadband Initiatives Program
BLS	Bureau of Labor Statistics
BTOP	Broadband Technology Opportunities Program
CIPA	Children's Internet Protection Act
CTC	community technology centers
DMCA	Digital Millennium Copyright Act
E-rate	education rate
FBI	Federal Bureau of Investigation
FCC	Federal Communications Commission
FDLC	Federal Depository Library Council
FDLP	Federal Depository Library Program
GPO	Government Printing Office

HCI	human computer interaction
ICT	information and communication technologies
ICT4D	information and communications technologies for development
IFLA	International Federation of Library Associations and Institutions
IMLS	Institute of Museum and Library Services
iPAC	Information Policy and Access Center
ISP	Internet service provider
ITU	International Telecommunication Union
LAP	Library Awareness Program
LGBTQ	lesbian, gay, bisexual, transgender, and questioning
LIS	library and information science
LSC	Legal Services Corporation
LSTA	Library Services and Technology Act
MLIS	master of library and information science
MLS	master of library science
NCSC	National Center for State Courts
NFIL	National Forum on Information Literacy
NGO	nongovernmental organization
NSL	national security letter
NTIA	National Telecommunications and Information Administration
OWS	Occupy Wall Street
PLG	Progressive Librarians Guild
ROI	return on investment
RUS	Rural Utilities Service
SOPA	Stop Online Piracy Act
SRLN	Self-Represented Litigation Network
UDHR	Universal Declaration of Human Rights
ULC	Urban Libraries Council
UN	United Nations
UNESCO	United Nations Educational, Scientific and Cultural Organization
USF	Universal Service Fund

Preface

Over the past several years, the authors of this book have taught, and in some cases cotaught, two graduate courses that are unique to the College of Information Studies at the University of Maryland: Information and Human Rights, and Inclusion, Literacy, and the Public Good. The former focuses on the nature of information within human rights, the rights dependent on information, the social justice issues raised by information, and the ways in which information professionals can support the implementation of these rights and advocate for policies that better support and extend these rights for their communities. In the latter, the goal of the class is to explore the ways in which information professionals are educators and social service professionals who specialize in information, emphasizing the use of the Internet to teach and provide innovative services to community members.

Both of these courses offer a window into the ways in which the profession of librarianship has matured and evolved at amazing speed. We challenge the students in these classes at the University of Maryland to directly engage these changes and explore the ways in which the issues will shape their careers. Certainly, a good percentage of people still decide to get a master of library science (MLS), master of library and information science (MLIS), or similar degree because they want to spend their time around books, reading materials, or other arcane collections. Anyone who reviews applications to library and information science (LIS) degree programs can still expect to see a decent number of essays that talk about wanting to be a librarian because of a love for reading or a desire to spend time around old books. However, an increasing number of students are entering LIS degree programs looking to devote their careers to providing better community services and to becoming change agents in their communities. In the pre-Internet era, libraries traditionally responded to changing populations through changes in their materials selection policies, their locations, their services, and their outreach to community groups (Shoham, 1984). Now, not only must libraries respond to changes in their communities in many more ways, they are also acting as change agents to improve their communities in many ways that were not previously possible.

Students taking these two classes generally come from the second population of students, and many immediately turn their class projects into new programs at the libraries where they work, new ways of teaching specific skills or literacies, or even new services for their communities on their own time. Projects from the classes that have become a reality in short order range from lessons for innovative approaches to teaching computer skills in multilingual environments, to story time sessions for young children on the autism spectrum, to maker spaces for children with disabilities, to a community archive for Korean American immigrants, among many others. It is impossible to teach these classes and mentor these students without being deeply impressed by the commitment of people in our field to use the knowledge and skills they have acquired to help others overcome barriers and to build stronger communities.

The future of public, academic, school, and special libraries and the work that they do lies in this space of being an actively engaged, information-enabled community center. The social roles and responsibilities of libraries have expanded greatly in the past few years, with libraries now serving as the one place of free public Internet access and support in many communities, providing digital literacy and digital inclusion classes, providing a gateway to education and employment, supporting social services and e-government, and serving emergency response roles. As a result, librarianship is increasingly becoming an information-enabled social service and education profession. Libraries facilitate learning in a range of ways—bridging the skills of librarians and the capacities of the technology in libraries—through "Ready to Read" initiatives, homework help services, support for online coursework, summer reading programs, small business development centers, and maker spaces with 3-D printers. Through technology availability, digital literacy courses, and other services, libraries teach and enable individuals to participate in and interact with a growing digital community. For a great many individuals, the library—along with the technology access, digital literacy, and digital inclusion provided within—has become central to being able to become educated, find employment, build a small business, become civically engaged, and participate in social media, among much else.

As communities face increasing challenges and opportunities in education, workforce development, health and wellness, environment, and other key areas, libraries have begun to play growing roles in meeting these challenges. They have seized opportunities in increasingly diverse communities to develop unique programs and innovative partnerships, often in combination with other public and nonprofit service agencies that also are dealing with dwindling budgets. The resulting programs include the creation of safe spaces for disadvantaged tweens, the provision of access to community health nurses, the establishment of immigration centers, the creation of legal assistance tools for self-represented litigants, and the delivery of fresh foods to food deserts, among many other vital contributions to their communities. In a few exceptional cases, libraries have even expanded the type of library to meet unique community needs. In Camden, New Jersey, the Rutgers University campus has a combination academic library and public library to serve four large public schools near the campus. Local high school students can use the public library on the lower floors for everyday needs, but they also have access to the academic library on the upper floors for more detailed research questions.

Whether or not current library professionals have taken time to individually ponder the implications of these changes in roles and expectations for libraries and the amazing contributions they make to their communities, these changes have occurred. Elsewhere, we have asserted that libraries are a completely unique kind of good that serves individuals, communities, and the society as a whole. The more money a community puts into a library, the more results the community can expect from the library (Jaeger, Gorham, Bertot, & Sarin, 2014). This attribute is very rare among what are known as public goods, the things that can benefit everyone in the community. Most public goods—from parks to traffic lights to lighthouses—have a discernable upper limit on how much they can support the community. Unlike other public goods, there is no upper bound on what a library can do for its community with sufficient funding. For that reason, we have suggested that libraries label themselves as a *community good* (Jaeger, Gorham, Bertot, & Sarin, 2014). The human rights and social justice functions of libraries are what truly make each public, school, academic, and special library a community good.

As individuals increasingly rely on information and communication technologies (ICTs) for many important life activities, it becomes all the more important for them to develop the skills to use them efficiently and effectively. The ability for any other organization or thing to be a public good is at least partially dependent upon librarians' ability to meet the community needs related to digital literacy and digital inclusion. Being the facilitators and educators of Internet access, digital literacy, and digital inclusion makes libraries a vital part of being a student, being a citizen, finding social services, seeking employment, and much else for many members of every community. Collaborating with other service agencies and organizations to meet specific community needs allows libraries to use their unique skills and resources to help address community problems that might otherwise go untended.

During her tenure as president of the American Library Association (ALA), Marilyn Miller stated, "ALA has a long tradition of supporting human rights and intellectual freedom" (M. Miller, 1993, p. 222). Though we have not historically labeled our activities in libraries using the language of human rights and social justice, it is exactly what we do in the age of the Internet. Many widely accepted human rights are dependent on or at least facilitated by Internet access, digital literacy, and digital inclusion. As the institution that guarantees access, literacy, and inclusion for diverse groups and also advocates for laws and policies that support these principles, libraries are central to human rights. "Those aspects of librarianship that commit librarians to serve democracy and human rights are what make the discipline essential to the survival of the human spirit" (McCook & Phenix, 2006, p. 25). And, as one of the few social institutions that fosters equality based on laws and policies, libraries are also central to social justice. Social justice "is activated as librarians work to provide all community members with inclusive services" (McCook, 2011, p. 67).

This book is intended to help librarians better understand and articulate their roles in promoting human rights and social justice, as well as to educate policy makers, government officials, professionals in other fields, and researchers in other disciplines about the contributions of libraries to human rights and social justice. Claiming our already ongoing roles related to human rights and social justice will help others to understand the unique and irreplaceable contributions of public, school, academic, and special libraries and the importance of enacting policies and funding decisions that support these contributions. It is time that we make clear that we are a community good, that we are central to supporting and protecting human rights and social justice, and that we have a very significant set of contributions to continue to make as technology becomes ever more central to people's lives. As was wisely noted by an author four decades ago: "If libraries do not exist ultimately to improve the quality of life, what do they exist for?" (Jordan, 1975, p. 62). By weaving together issues of libraries, information, human rights, and social justice, this book will help to illuminate these interrelationships and encourage society to value the true breadth and depth of libraries' contributions to their communities.

Acknowledgments

This is the third book that we have written for Rowman & Littlefield in the space of about eighteen months, and they have been tremendously supportive throughout this pretty intense bout of writing. Charles Harmon, Robert Hayunga, Lara Graham, and particularly Martin Dillon have been enthusiastic, timely, and helpful in every way that an academic author could want.

We are also grateful to all of our colleagues at the Information Policy and Access Center (iPAC) at the University of Maryland. Most of their names can be found sprinkled among the citations in this book, which reflects the delightfully collaborative atmosphere in which we are privileged to work. Their various insights through countless discussions and collaborations have been most valuable as we conceived of and wrote this book. We'd particularly like to thank Karen Kettnich, Lindsay Sarin, and Kaitlin Peterson, our coconspirators in putting out *Library Quarterly* every few months. Insights we've had while working on the journal have been central to the decision to write this book.

As with the majority of the eleven books he has written over the past twelve years, Paul would like to thank his mother, Carol, for always being enthusiastic about reading and commenting on drafts of these books. And as has been the case in many previous books, he'd like to thank his devoted bevy of cats for being excellent company while writing (or pretending to write, but instead playing with the cats).

Natalie would like to thank her husband, Brian, for his patience, love, and rare ability to help manage her type A tendencies. She would also like to thank her brother, Nicholas, for the thorough education in argumentation and her parents, Matt and Debbie, for the lessons on finding solutions—both necessary skills for writing a book!

Ursula would like to thank her "three boys" for being self-sufficient enough to take care of things during the past couple of years of book and dissertation writing. She also thanks the Honorable Paul Mannes, who encouraged her to think about access to information and social justice (probably unbeknownst to him) years before she started writing about these issues.

And as always, we are most grateful to the readers of this book for spending time with our ideas.

Chapter One

Introduction

The concept of human rights is the belief that all individuals deserve certain equal rights as members of society, while the implementation of human rights is tied to specific legal and policy mechanisms that promote equality. For human rights to be effectively implemented, they depend on systems of social justice, the social and societal structures that foster equality based on the laws and policies. The language of human rights and social justice is employed to express the need for fairness, equality, respect, and equity (Sensoy & DiAngelo, 2012). The lack of human rights is tied to "low life expectancy, social exclusion, ill health, illiteracy, dependency, and effective enslavement" (Pogge, 2005, p. 1). The achievement of equality, however, is not just a means of finding a way to accomplish equal distribution of resources or opportunities, as different needs and social contexts may require greater interventions for certain groups to achieve equality (Cramme & Diamond, 2009; Nieto, 2010). Together, these structures form the basis of the protection and fostering of equity in society. Increasingly, a central aspect of equality is information.

As information and related technologies have become increasingly essential to education, employment, social interaction, and civic participation, greater focus has been placed on the idea that information can be seen as a necessary human right and a core part of social justice. Information intersects with human rights and social justice in several significant ways, including

- the wide range of social, cultural, economic, legal, and political forces shaping information and rights;
- impacts of rights on information professions, practices, standards, and cultural institutions; and

1

• considerations of justice in information access and use by different populations.

Arguments thus have been made that information access, information literacy, intellectual freedom, freedom of expression, and other information behaviors fall under the category of rights and justice in the age of the Internet (e.g., Duffy, 2001; Hoffman, 2001; Jaeger, Bertot, & Gorham, 2013; Jaeger, Bertot, Thompson, Katz, & DeCoster, 2012; Mathiesen, 2013; McCook & Phenix, 2006; Phenix & McCook, 2005; Stinnett, 2009; Suarez, 2007).

To see how information is a significant and pressing issue in this area, an examination of the United Nations' Universal Declaration of Human Rights (UDHR) is instructive. The antecedents of current information technologies were still fairly new when the United Nations (UN) issued the UDHR in 1948. Since its passage, however, the idea of human rights has been evolving and adapting to social, cultural, and technological change. Though the desktop computer, the Internet, and mobile devices were developed long after the UDHR was originally drafted, many of the principles articulated in the UDHR are directly related to information, communication, and technology; many more rely on information, communication, and technology to support the principles. Most items directly stated as rights are now either entirely dependent on or greatly enabled by information access and digital literacy, including such major activities as education, employment, and civic participation. As examples, freedom of speech, press, assembly, and expression are far more practicable when involving a literate populace with access to ICTs. Human rights to education and development are possible without access to and use of ICTs, but they are much more effective with the technologies.

Article 19 of the UDHR most explicitly deals with issues of information, enshrining rights to "freedom of opinion and expression" and to "seek, receive and impart information and ideas through any media," as well as freedom from "interference" in seeking and exchanging information and ideas. Based on this article and many other parts of the UDHR, the ability to access and use the Internet for purposes of education and expression has been identified as a human right in many quarters. Not long after use of the World Wide Web became commonplace, scholars of law, information, technology, and education began making arguments in favor of universal Internet access as a necessary part of human rights (e.g., Brophy & Halpin, 1999; Lievrouw & Farb, 2003; Mart, 2003; McIver, Birdsall, & Rasmussen, 2003; Willingham, 2008). As Internet-enabled technologies have become more mobile and omnipresent—and vital to education, employment, civic engagement, communication, and entertainment—these arguments have matured into assertions that the abilities to successfully access and to successfully use the Internet are both human rights (e.g., Jaeger, 2013; Koepfler, Mascaro, &

Jaeger, 2014; Lyons, 2011; Sturges & Gastinger, 2010; Thompson, Jaeger, Taylor, Subramaniam, & Bertot, 2014).

In the past fifteen years, arguments have also been made for the central role of educational and cultural heritage institutions—including public libraries, public schools, academic libraries, archives, and museums—in ensuring human rights related to the Internet in an age so dependent on information and technology (e.g., Duffy, 2001; Hoffman, 2001; McCook & Phenix, 2006; Phenix & McCook, 2005; Stinnett, 2009; Suarez, 2007; Thompson et al., 2014). The Progressive Librarians Guild (PLG) in particular has advocated for human rights and social justice issues for decades. However, library literature contains many discussions of human rights and social justice issues as very small-scale activities—such as a particular service or program or outreach or issue—but these are rarely labeled as human rights and social justice activities, and discussions of the large-scale human rights and social justice activities of libraries are rather limited.

The ALA, the International Federation of Library Associations and Institutions (IFLA), the United Nations Education, Scientific and Cultural Organization (UNESCO), and other information professional and governmental organizations have adopted Article 19 and the principles of information access as a human right into their bylaws and policies. Even the Internet Society, an organization that bills itself as "the world's trusted independent source of leadership for Internet policy, technology standards, and future development," declared the ability to use the Internet to be a human right in 2011.

Also in 2011, a UN report explicitly discussed Internet access as being central to supporting Article 19 of the UDHR and enabling many other aspects of the UDHR (Human Rights Council, 2011). While the report never explicitly labels Internet access to be a human right, many media outlets interpreted the report as doing so (e.g., Olivarez-Giles, 2011). The IFLA-led *Lyon Declaration on Access to Information and Development* (2014) called upon the UN to make information literacy and digital inclusion central to their human rights and development agendas, building upon the assertions made in the 2006 Alexandria Proclamation for the UN and individual nations to make information literacy a central part of their goals (UNESCO, IFLA, and National Forum on Information Literacy [NFIL], 2006). Such statements reflect the ideas that have come to be known as information and communications technologies for development (ICT4D), which encourage the use of ICTs to promote community development and the growth of education, health care, and general welfare (Zelenika & Pierce, 2013).

The assertion that Internet access is a human right by many different professional groups, nonprofit organizations, and international agencies presents a clear opportunity to firmly place Internet access as an issue of human rights and social justice in the minds of members of the public, politicians, and policy makers. Based on a wealth of research about libraries, their practices and services, the public policies that impact them, and the professional stances and beliefs of librarians, this book presents the first comprehensive, research-based vision of libraries as core institutions of both human rights and social justice.

Libraries have long served many vital roles in ensuring access and equity in their communities. While these activities have not typically been described in terms of human rights and social justice, long-standing library activities—like job seeking help, literacy courses, children's story time, computer classes, and many other library functions—are in fact social service activities that are designed to promote social inclusion and social equity. Libraries have also been at the forefront of major political issues related to inclusion and equity, with many libraries taking a leadership role in the civil rights movement and, more recently, the struggles to promote freedom of expression and to challenge censorship. They remain committed to fulfilling the needs of the full spectrum of the communities that they serve, from the individual to different groups in the community to the entire service population. Whereas many traditional public spaces in communities—the town square, the public gardens, the community market, and other places that serve to foster interaction among community members—have become less visible or ceased to exist, the library continues to be an extremely important public space devoted to promoting inclusion and equity.

The historical continuity of librarianship is not tied to the objects that contain information, like books, records, computers, and e-books. The continuity lies in providing access to information, ensuring that patrons can use and understand the information, and advocating for the unmet needs of their patrons. Issues of equity are at the heart of much of this evolution that has occurred over the past one hundred years. The engagement of libraries in information provision, services, educational programming, advocacy for inclusion, and community outreach are all aspects of an unarticulated but central focus on rights and justice issues. The authors of this book have already argued that the historical starting point of public libraries as an institution fostering human rights and social justice in the United States can be seen as occurring during the influx of new immigrant populations to the United States during and shortly after World War I (Gorham, Bertot, Jaeger, & Taylor, 2013). To help these immigrants, public libraries quickly developed English-language courses for adults, employed children's story time to teach English to children, began offering job training classes and job seeking classes, emphasized health information, and even created resources to help new immigrants find housing.

The social roles and responsibilities of libraries have expanded even more in the past few years, with public libraries now serving as the one place of free public Internet access and support within their communities, providing digital literacy and digital inclusion classes, supporting e-government, serving emergency response roles, and becoming increasingly involved in the provision of social services and education. The years of the Great Recession have emphatically solidified the rights and justice focus of all types of libraries, with many creating programs to meet pressing community needs. While librarians have often struggled to meet these overwhelming new needs, the range of innovative programs and partnerships created in response to these needs is nothing short of amazing. Librarians are creating new homework help services, hiring social workers, providing access to community health nurses, establishing immigration centers, teaching patrons about eating organic and meeting specific dietary needs, and facilitating the delivery of fresh foods to food deserts, among many other vital contributions to their communities (Bertot & Jaeger, 2012; Gorham, Bertot, Jaeger, & Taylor, 2013; Jaeger, Taylor, Bertot, Perkins, & Wahl, 2012; N. G. Taylor, Gorham, Jaeger, & Bertot, 2014). In other words, libraries are continually adapting and innovating to meet the basic needs of their communities.

These services are not confined to public libraries. Rather, the library as an institution serves as a place of community and continuity, with all types of libraries working to ensure equitable access to information, education, technology, and services. As Leonard Kniffel has correctly noted, "The children using the libraries represented by the American Association of School Librarians today are the students who will be using the libraries represented by the Association of College and Research Libraries tomorrow, and all of them are the Public Library Association's patrons of the future. These are not separate universes. United, they are the roadmap for a productive lifetime of reading, learning, and fulfillment" (2005, p. 33).

The support for and provision of rights and justice—education, employment, civic participation, digital inclusion, social services, public spaces, digital literacy, and other community needs—are the defining issues for the present and future of public, school, and academic libraries. While interest in issues of human rights and social justice as they relate to libraries and information has been growing recently, it remains an area that has received little attention in print. Thus far, only a few books that have been published are devoted to the issue of libraries and human rights or libraries and social justice.

Toni Samek's 2007 book *Librarianship and Human Rights*, by its own admission, "is not meant to be a scholarly book" (p. xxiv) and devotes more than three-quarters of its text to definitions and examples of social actions taken by libraries. While such a focus on examples from practice is extremely valuable in providing ideas to other libraries, it does not address in detail the broad social and political context in conjunction with the professional considerations. *Beyond Article 19: Libraries and Social and Cultural Rights* (Edwards & Edwards, 2010) is an exceptionally brief volume that only focuses on cultural rights issues in very specific contexts. It does not address the broader issues of human rights for libraries and librarianship, nor does it address any issues of social justice. *Public Libraries and Social Justice* (Pateman & Vincent, 2010), published in the United Kingdom, gives limited consideration to the larger issues of social justice and does not address human rights. In spite of the title, it is primarily about social exclusion issues; as with the Samek book, it is a valuable tool for improving practice, but does not focus much on the broader picture. An encyclopedia article on "Social Justice in Library and Information Science" devotes the largest section of text to arguing that the field has only been able to bring "moderate socially progressive changes in their communities," but then notes new technologies offer opportunities to considerably increase the social justice impact of libraries (Mehra, Rioux, & Albright, 2009, p. 4829).

The most thorough attempts to engage the concepts as both sociopolitical and professional issues appear in some recent books on related topics, meriting discussions in Kathleen de la Pena McCook's 2011 *Introduction to Public Librarianship* (2nd ed.) and two recent books by the authors of this book (Jaeger, Gorham, Bertot, & Sarin, 2014; Thompson et al., 2014). This very brief review of the related literature demonstrates that the connections between information and human rights and information and social justice have not received a great deal of attention.

Subtle changes are occurring now, though, as the ALA's 2013 *Declaration for the Right to Libraries* references the UDHR before asserting that "libraries are essential to a democratic society" (ALA, 2013a). The theme of the annual conference of the Association of Library and Information Science Educators (ALISE) for 2015 is libraries and social justice, and both *Library Trends* and *Library Quarterly* have special issues coming out in 2015 on the topic of libraries and social justice. Wikipedia even has a page devoted to "Librarianship and Human Rights in the United States" (Wikipedia, 2014). The focus, however, tends to either be on rights *or* justice, rather than on how they are interrelated and both necessary for true equality in terms of information. In spite of the limited way in which they are often discussed in other venues, the increase in attention to these issues indicates that this is a perfect time for a book that examines the continuum of libraries, information, human rights, and social justice.

Along with previous works in this area bifurcating human rights and social justice, these discussions also often tend to focus only on one part of the field of librarianship, most of them public libraries. This book contends that the inherent actions of librarians and the intrinsic nature of libraries are based in human rights and social justice. While the size of the community served and the funding models differ—as do the relationships with patrons—across types of libraries, they all offer access, education, literacy, services, and inclusion in relation to some body of information to their service populations.

It is easier to see these roles in public libraries; they are open to all and their successes and struggles become public discourse in their communities. However, school and academic libraries serve their student patrons—who are usually from a wide range of backgrounds in terms of socioeconomic status, education, information literacy, and digital inclusion—in all of the same ways that public libraries do. Helping a patron meet a major life need, such as finding needed health information, in any of these libraries may occur through a different process and may involve different levels of material, but it is the same act of teaching digital literacy and supporting the patron in reaching and becoming educated about needed life information. Special libraries vary more than any other kind of library, but they too all provide inclusion in information to some specific population. In many cases, that specific population includes a section of the general public, such as a public law library.

In the case of all types of libraries, the interaction is ultimately about transformation, not transaction. As such, all have roles to play in human rights and social justice for their specific patrons and their specific service communities. This book uses examples from all of these different libraries to illustrate the arguments. More examples come from public libraries and school libraries than the other types of libraries, due to both their being the most common types of libraries and their serving the broadest segments of society.

While this book is about libraries, it should be noted that archives also play key roles in human rights and social justice. As with libraries, these issues are also beginning to receive more attention among archivists. In 2014, *Archival Science* published a special double issue on archives and human rights, focusing on the roles of archives in "the creation, preservation, and use of records documenting human rights crises" (Caswell, 2014, p. 207). Some archives have a long history of preserving the record of human rights and social justice activities and abuses (Montgomery, 1996; Stinnett, 2009). These archival materials have been used to not only educate and provide material for histories about rights and justice issues, they have also been used in court proceedings to help resolve rights and justice issues (Lindsay, 2001). Stronger proponents of archives as human rights organizations have called for "archives to reconceptualize their roles as activists for the protections of human rights" (Stinnett, 2009, p. 10). While issues related to archives as institutions of human rights and social justice clearly merit greater discussion, an exploration of these issues is beyond the scope of this book.

As the library profession is already focused on equity through information, an important part of this book will be an exploration of the reasons that librarians do not generally discuss themselves and their work in terms of the social and societal implications. The book will also discuss the implications for these choices, and the stances that could be taken in advocacy and policy debates to better articulate what libraries actually do in these areas. This last point is particularly significant, as libraries currently fill many essential functions in fostering equity and inclusion and promoting rights that no other social institution can fulfill. If librarians better understand and can more strongly articulate their position as an institution of human rights and social justice, they will be better placed to proactively meet their community needs, argue for support, and embrace their wholly unique contributions to the lives of patrons and their communities.

MEANINGS OF HUMAN RIGHTS AND SOCIAL JUSTICE

While chapter 2 will examine the concepts, definitions, instruments, and implications of human rights and social justice in detail, it is important to introduce here some discussion of the meanings given to human rights and social justice as they will be used in this book. The ways in which the terms are used in different fields varies greatly, with the field of library science oddly shying away from using the words, notwithstanding the fact that libraries do a great deal of work to promote human rights and social justice.

The term "human rights" was a creation of the twentieth century, but many scholars have looked to earlier days to find origins for its underlying principles. Many fields offer perspectives on human rights: law, politics, education, religion, economics, communication, sociology, psychology, and transportation, among others (Goodman, Jinks, & Woods, 2012). Across these fields, human rights as a term is widely varied in meaning, influenced by traditions and cultures of religion, law, philosophy, and other bodies of knowledge. "Claims are presented, criticisms are formulated by invoking human rights. More often than not, however, it remains unclear what connotation is attached to that concept" (Tomuschat, 2003, p. 1). Most discussions of human rights rely on language of either philosophy to provide justification or law to promote implementation, but a cross-disciplinary way to think of human rights is as legal structures created to empower individuals and communities against persecution and injustice (Evans, 1998).

The first clear statement of a set of tangible human rights—which she identifies as "birthrights"—may have been Mary Wollstonecraft's 1790 anti-poverty treatise *A Vindication of the Rights of Men*, which attacked the wrongs of social hierarchies, poverty, economic inequality, and state oppression in England (Blau & Moncada, 2006). As part of philosophical arguments, the idea of human rights has long been a part of debates whether people are born with natural rights, a position most notably advocated by John Locke. Others believe rights only exist if allowed and protected by larger community and social structures, such as logical positivist philosopher Jeremy Bentham. The Declaration of Independence of the United States evidences clear adherence to the former rather than the latter, while limiting those to whom such rights were available.

Discussions of human rights also reflect perceptions not just of the meaning of "rights," but of the meaning of "human" as well. Some believe that human rights reflect the best of human nature, arguing that human rights "cannot be distinguished from the origins of humans" and they are what "distinguishes mankind from other animals" (Blau & Moncada, 2006, p. 12). Such statements are focusing on the positive side of human rights—society offering legal guarantees of equity and equality. On the other hand, some conceive of human rights as protections from the continual inequality, violence, and chaos that so often define human interactions. Focusing on the darker side of human rights, this point of view characterizes them as "profound and disturbing" as "they tend to strike at our very core and make us confront difficult and discomforting issues" (Lauren, 2011, p. 5).

Within this book, we are most interested in the practical side of human rights, and thus will avoid most of the philosophical discussions of the term. Human rights scholar Anthony Woodiwiss offers a very practical definition of human rights that serves this purpose well: "a legally enforceable set of expectations as to how others, most obviously the state, should behave toward the rights bearers" (2005, p. xi). As noted earlier, the focus herein is on human rights as the belief that all individuals deserve certain equal rights as members of society, enforced by specific legal and policy mechanisms that promote such equality.

Social justice has proved to be a similarly thorny term. The term originates from the writings of philosopher Luigi Taparelli, who coined the term in the 1840s to describe the tensions between the rights of individuals and the rights of individuals when they form a society (Barry, 1989; Behr, 2003). Modern thinking about social justice has been heavily determined by John Rawls's articulation of the concept in his epic 1971 treatise, *A Theory of Justice*: "the way in which major social institutions distribute fundamental rights and duties and determine the division of advantages from social cooperation" (p. 6). As with human rights, many fields have put forward differing approaches and meanings of the term, and schools from different fields have also looked for antecedents for the modern articulations. Some believe that the search for social justice can be seen as beginning with Socrates and Plato (Baldwin, 1966), heavily influenced by the fact that in the ancient Greek language, "justice" and "equality" were the same word (Vlastos, 1962).

Economists have considered social justice for more than five decades, discussing the ways in which the law supports equality of economic opportunities for individuals and for enterprise, as well as exploring the impacts of issues of economic policy on equality of economic opportunity (i.e., issues of property rights, welfare, wages, wealth and material distribution, and prices) (Baldwin, 1966). Psychologists and sociologists have also been considering the concept for many decades. For psychologists, social justice "involves efforts at understanding the causes and consequences of subjective justice judgments" (Tyler, Boeckmann, Smith, & Huo, 1997, p. 5). Justice is evaluated subjectively by people, based upon their perceptions of fairness: "How people feel and behave in social settings is strongly shaped by judgments about justice and injustice" (Tyler, Boeckmann, Smith, & Huo, 1997, p. 6). These perceptions, which are often tied to political attitudes, biases, and beliefs about other groups, are often reflected in feelings of anger, envy, depression, outrage, and self-esteem. Other long-established ways of conceiving of social justice define it as follows:

- "Essentially a quality of the behavior of one man to another, that is of man in society, so that all justice is social justice" (Baldwin, 1966, p. 1)
- "The problem of justice in society or of a just society" (Brandt, 1962, p. v)
- An influence on social dynamics and the evolution of society (Boulding, 1962)
- A set of both formal rules (legal, political, and economic) and informal rules (moral sanctions and conventions) (Frankena, 1962, p. 2)

An oddity of social justice discourse is that it is a concept that is difficult to oppose, given its flexibility to accommodate different beliefs and perspectives. "Everybody is in favor of social justice, almost by definition" (Burchardt & Craig, 2008, p. 1).

Over time, social justice research has moved from a focus on relative deprivation (satisfaction with distribution) to distributive justice (outcome distributions) to procedural justice (fairness in resolving conflicts and making adjustments) to redistributive justice (how people react to the breaking of social rules) (Tyler, Boeckmann, Smith, & Huo, 1997). Yet, the extent to which social justice is dependent on the individual, the society, or a combination of the two remains unsettled. Rawls placed much of the burden on the state to ensure social justice and much less on the individual, and scholarly debates since that time have continued to focus on those divisions (Burchardt & Craig, 2008). Many discussions of human rights from a range of perspectives now directly incorporate considerations of social justice as well (Jackson, 2005).

As with human rights, this book will emphasize the practical nature of social justice. We will focus on social justice as the social and societal structures that foster equality based on laws and policies. For human rights to be effectively implemented, they depend on systems of social justice; for systems of social justice to be relevant, they need to be built upon a frame-work of recognized human rights.

MEANINGS OF ACCESS, POLICY, LITERACY, AND INCLUSION

A more straightforward task is establishing the meaning of some other key terms—ones from the study of libraries and information—within the context of this book. There will be much discussion in this book about issues of digital literacy and digital inclusion as being essential to providing informa-tion in human rights and social justice contexts. For the purposes of this book, the ability to use the Internet to meet information needs will be labeled *digital literacy*, while access to the Internet in order to successfully apply the skills of digital literacy will be discussed in terms of *digital inclusion* (Thompson et al., 2014). While each of these terms can carry many different connotations, the above definitions will guide the discussion herein and will be expanded upon in subsequent chapters.

When discussing these issues in the context of library or government efforts, digital inclusion will be mainly an issue of outreach as a means to empower underserved and marginalized populations. Rather than distinguish between the digitally excluded, the digitally unengaged, digital inequality, and so forth, this book discusses digital inclusion in terms of the means developed by governmental and nongovernmental entities to close the digital divide and promote human rights, social inclusion, and digital literacy. Addi-tionally, the term *public policy* will be used to indicate decisions and actions by the government to impact—or at least attempt to impact—public prob-lems (Jaeger, Gorham, Bertot, & Sarin, 2014). Policies include "legislation, executive orders, agency memos, rulemaking, signing statements, and a range of other measures at the government's disposal" (Jaeger, Bertot, & Gorham, 2013, p. 62).

The most complicated concept from LIS research that needs to be defined at the outset of the book is *access*. This book discusses information access in terms of the tripartite model of access: physical, intellectual, and social (Bur-nett, Jaeger, & Thompson, 2008). *Physical access* is generally viewed as access to the document or other form embodying information, be it conveyed through print, electronic, verbal, or another means of communication—liter-ally the process of getting to the information that is being sought (Svenonius, 2000). The vast majority of discourse on information access tends to focus on physical issues, such as the physical structures that contain information, the electronic structures that contain information, and the paths that are traveled to get to information (Jaeger & Bowman, 2005). Issues of physical access relate to the location and format of the entity containing information, and the conditions, technologies, or abilities required for reaching that entity. Such issues are often readily identifiable and revolve around the questions of whether people can get into the location that houses the information and then reach the specific information that they seek.

Physical access is of utmost importance; without it, no other type of access is possible (Jaeger & Bowman, 2005). However, while it is a necessary prerequisite, mere physical access is not sufficient for full access. For instance, "it is a common, but mistaken, assumption that access to technology equals access to information" (McCreadie & Rice, 1999, p. 51). The ability of a user to get to information and the ability of that user to employ information to accomplish particular goals are very different (Culnan, 1983, 1984, 1985). As a result, the physical aspects of information access cannot be considered without also considering the intellectual aspects of information access.

Intellectual access can be understood as the accessing of the information itself after physical access has been obtained (Svenonius, 2000). It revolves around the ability to understand how to get to and, in particular, how to understand the information itself once it has been physically obtained. Much less research has examined issues of intellectual access than of physical access. Issues of intellectual access involve understanding how the information is presented to people seeking information, as well as the impact the presentation has on the process of information seeking (Jaeger & Bowman, 2005, p. 67). As a result, for an item to provide information equally to all, it must be able to produce similar outcomes or results for any user, regardless of any disadvantages that the user might have. Intellectual access to a particular item of information, however, is often not available on an equal basis to all who seek it.

Many individual issues unique to each user influence intellectual access, as it hinges on the user understanding the information once it has been physically accessed. Factors that can affect intellectual access include information seeking behavior, language, dialect, education, literacy, technological skill, cognitive ability, disability, vocabulary, and social elements, such as norms and values. Each of these factors has the potential to influence whether an information seeker can access the information contained in a source. Intellectual access requires the ability to understand the information in a source, which, in turn, requires the cognitive ability to understand the source, the ability to read the language in which the source is written, and the knowledge of the specific vocabulary that is used. Intellectual access also requires knowledge of the use of any necessary technology to access a source, such as telephones, computers, mobile devices, search engines, electronic databases, or the Internet.

In many cases, the discussion of information access ends with physical and intellectual access to information. Many assume that, if both physical and intellectual access are present, the individual should have no problem becoming fully informed. However, in terms of actual information access, this assumption fails to take into account one additional layer that is omnipresent although too often overlooked: *social access*. This third and most abstract aspect of information access captures the idea that, simply because one *can* physically and intellectually access needed information, it does not necessarily follow that they *do* access that information or that all users interpret the information in the same way. The social layer of information access has been well established in research, through studies of the influences of social trust, social motivation, and social inclusion on information behavior (e.g., Chatman, 1987, 1990, 1991; Dervin & Greenberg, 1972; Rogers, 1995), social and cultural norms that influence information availability and use within the social context (e.g., Burnett, Besant, & Chatman, 2001; Chatman, 1996, 1999, 2000), social grounds or locations where information is accessed through interpersonal interactions (e.g., Fisher & Naumer, 2005), and social networks and information access (e.g., Granovetter, 1973, 1983). Social information access has also been explored in terms of normative behavior and the social sphere (Burnett & Jaeger, 2012; Jaeger & Burnett, 2010).

Because of the complexity of the concept of access and its constituent parts, and the importance of this concept to any examination of information as an issue of human rights and social justice, the foregoing definition of access is considerably more detailed than the other definitions provided in this chapter. Unfortunately, the discourse about information and human rights primarily focuses on physical access to information, and fails to consider the capabilities of individuals to use the information (Britz, Hoffman, Ponelis, Zimmer, & Lor, 2013). Without achieving equal access to information—all three levels of access—the role that information can play in the fulfillment of human rights and social justice is limited.

STRUCTURE OF THE BOOK

Exploring the intersections of information, human rights, and social justice from a range of perspectives, this book addresses library institutions (public, school, academic, and special libraries), library professionals, professional organizations, governments, and library patrons. The key aspects of information as an issue of rights and justice that are examined include

- information, human rights, and social justice in social, cultural, economic, legal, educational, and political contexts;
- information as a right in specific contexts, such as access, literacy, inclusion, behavior, expression, and intellectual freedom, among others;

- rights and justice in the context of different types of libraries (public, school, academic, and special);
- the impacts of law and policy on information as a tool of equity;
- historical roots of libraries as education and social service institutions and advocates for equity;
- factors that create information inequalities;
- factors that foster information equalities;
- information inequalities and disadvantaged populations;
- professional opportunities, challenges, and best practices related to rights and justice;
- implications for program development, assessment, advocacy, and policy engagement;
- the roles of professional codes and standards;
- the impacts of technological development and change on information as a right;
- the impacts of technological change on perceptions of rights and justice; and
- the influences of law, policy, technology, and professional standards on the development of rights and justice related to information.

These topics are discussed through legal, policy, social, cultural, and economic lenses. Issues are examined both in terms of efforts to support equity in communities as a whole and the efforts intended to promote equity in specific disadvantaged or marginalized populations, such as the homeless, immigrants, people with disabilities, and the socioeconomically disadvantaged. Many examples of the issues discussed are drawn from the original research that the authors have conducted.

Following this introductory chapter, the remainder of the book explores the key themes identified above. Chapter 2 describes the historical evolution of the interrelationship among information, human rights, and social justice. Using the UDHR and the ALA's Bill of Rights to frame the discussion, it sets forth how information access, information literacy, intellectual freedom, freedom of expression, and related principles have been increasingly recognized as central to the advancement of human rights and social justice. Focusing on the role of libraries in this evolution, chapter 2 then examines the library profession's involvement in issues related to human rights and social justice throughout the twentieth and twenty-first centuries. This historical overview highlights libraries' roles in providing a wide range of social services to their surrounding communities, demonstrating how libraries' commitment to access to information can also be characterized as a commitment to the advancement of human rights and social justice. This overview therefore sets the stage for chapter 3's discussion of digital inclusion, access gaps, and libraries and chapter 4's discussion of the profession's current engagement in human rights and social justice issues.

Chapter 3 contextualizes the issue of libraries' roles in human rights and social justice by describing the current state of information, the Internet, and digital literacy as issues of human rights and social justice. The chapter will first discuss approaches that the U.S. government has taken to digital inclusion and digital literacy through policies, laws, regulations, and other instruments of government. The chapter then provides an overview of gaps in access that have been created by these government instruments, including an exploration of the ways in which these gaps affect populations differently, in many cases exacerbating existing social injustices.

Chapter 4 advances the concept of libraries "as institutions of rights and justice" by exploring libraries' current practices that promote social justice and human rights. Different types of libraries—public, school, academic, and special—are included in this discussion and examples illustrate the vast impact that libraries have on all types of communities. A key thread that is woven into this discussion is the relationship between libraries and their communities and the ways that libraries serve as the main (and often only) community information access point. By describing examples of innovative library programs and services, this chapter offers ample evidence of the fact that libraries are the most qualified institutions to promote and advance equality of access to information.

Having demonstrated in chapter 4 the various ways that libraries already act as institutions of human rights and social justice, chapter 5 then focuses on an important question: Why are libraries not promoted in these terms? The discussion explores two main reasons for this discrepancy, namely, the library community's perception of itself and the broader economic forces at play in this country. This discussion encompasses the historical development of perceptions about libraries from both inside and outside of the profession, professional principles that have been embraced by librarians, and engagement of issues beyond the library walls.

Chapter 6 highlights the ways in which a disconnect between what the field says it is, what society thinks it is, and what libraries actually do has often worked to impede the library community's ability to effectively engage in political discourse and policy making related to access to information. It focuses on discourse and actions undertaken by libraries in connection with a number of federal laws (including, but not limited to, the Children's Internet Protection Act [CIPA], the USA PATRIOT Act, and the Stop Online Piracy Act [SOPA]), as well as with ongoing policy debates surrounding issues such as net neutrality, the privatization of libraries, and the Federal Depository Library Program (FDLP). The chapter also examines the ways in which the framing of the issues that are central to these laws and policies impact (often adversely) the manner and level of the library profession's involvement.

Chapter 7 crystalizes the central thesis of the book—that libraries are already institutions of human rights and social justice in practice and should fully embrace this role in the policy, advocacy, and marketing arenas as well, or as we phrase it throughout the book, "becoming what they already are." To this end, the chapter explores the ways in which librarians, libraries, and library professional organizations can embrace, articulate, and advocate based on their prominent roles as social institutions dedicated to human rights and social justice.

Finally, chapter 8 serves to encapsulate the ways forward, recommending ways that the library profession can engage in the policy-making process. In addition, the chapter suggests ways in which librarians can frame discussions of current practices to better advocate for their roles in promoting social justice and human rights. The chapter concludes by considering the importance of creating and implementing more effective policies that can better assist libraries in their role as institutions that promote inclusion and equality.

Given that this book covers much new ground in weaving together existing literature and presenting the first comprehensive, research-based vision of libraries as core institutions of both human rights and social justice, it has been written to be widely accessible to all those in the field of LIS. This book is intended for professionals, students, educators, and researchers in all types of libraries, as they confront these issues on a daily basis. The ideas and suggestions in this book hopefully will help members of the library community understand where their roles related to human rights and social justice originate, how they fit within the broader policy context, how to improve their related services and practices, and how to advocate for better support of these roles.

Additionally, readers interested in an information studies approach to human rights and social justice from any number of other fields and professions will have an interest in this text. The book is written to be accessible to both professional and scholarly audiences, regardless of discipline. By drawing upon the work from a range of disciplines beyond LIS—including law, sociology, psychology, communications, public administration, philosophy, and governance—the themes in the book will resonate with readers from many perspectives. Throughout the book, key terms from these different fields are discussed and defined as needed to ensure that all readers understand broad concepts related to human rights, social justice, and ICTs from these different perspectives.

One of the main goals of the book is to help educate both people within the library field and those beyond it about the true roles and contributions of libraries in human rights and social justice. As such, this multidisciplinary focus will hopefully make the book be of interest to students and researchers within the disciplines of LIS, communications, education, media studies, and political science. It is written at a level to make it useful to undergraduate and postgraduate students, researchers, and policy makers. As more people begin to realize and consider the centrality of literacy, inclusion, human rights, and social justice in the information age, this book is meant to inform discussion of these issues in many different contexts.

BECOMING WHAT WE ALREADY ARE

A key theme throughout this book is that libraries—public, academic, school, and special—are institutions that are already deeply embedded in both human rights and social justice functions. Libraries provide the information access and digital literacy that are essential for most human rights, including education, work, interaction, civic participation, development, and mobility. At the same time, libraries are also part of the social justice infrastructure of society. As other parts of the public sphere have diminished or disappeared, the library stands as the primary institution of social inclusion and digital inclusion in most communities. They are instrumental in realizing the human rights ideals related to information by tying them to actual skills and the contexts in which to use those skills, such as taking courses online, doing homework, using e-government, seeking social services, or applying for jobs. Libraries concurrently provide information, means to access the information, training and education to understand the information, and social connections to apply the information.

It has been argued that libraries themselves should be seen as a human right (Mathiesen, 2013); however, the situation is far more complex. Simultaneously acting as an institution that facilitates both human rights and social justice places libraries in a unique and tremendously important position that librarians themselves have difficulty articulating. Thus far, unfortunately, libraries have not frequently framed their activities in the terminology of human rights or social justice, even though they are the organizations most focused on the good of the whole community and all of the individual members of the community. Often, when library activities are framed in terms of human rights and social justice, the focus is limited to topics such as the ways in which libraries can help other organizations or groups in their human rights and social justice activities (e.g., Gregory & Higgins, 2013; Morrone, 2014).

However, the human rights and social justice functions of libraries are absolutely definitional of what libraries have evolved into in the age of the Internet. Embracing and clearly articulating these existing roles and the accompanying terminology will enable libraries to better explain what they do and how they contribute to society, formulate ways to better help their patrons and their communities, and advocate for the support that they so desperately need.

Libraries do not need to try to change but rather only need to acknowledge what they are currently doing—becoming what they already are—so that their social and societal contributions are duly recognized by those who may not understand all that libraries currently do in this area. Libraries are so deeply ingrained as a beloved social institution that they have the opportunity to make great social changes in their current state. Positioning themselves as critical players within the realm of human rights and social justice will help drive their influence in promoting better laws and policies that foster inclusion, access, equity, and equality in the digital age.

This book serves as the culmination of what might be considered an accidental trilogy. In 2014, Rowman & Littlefield released two books—*Public Libraries, Public Policies, and Political Processes: Serving and Transforming Communities in Times of Economic and Political Constraint* and *Digital Literacy and Digital Inclusion: Information Policy and the Public Library*—that were cowritten by the authors of this book. Those two books each have a distinct topical focus that included some discussions of issues of human rights and social justice, but these discussions were limited to being part of the respective topics at hand.

However, it became abundantly clear in the writing of those books that the relevant human rights and social justice issues were so significant that they demanded deeper consideration. This book builds on the foundation of these other two books—with their focus on issues of inclusion, social service roles, policy, and advocacy—to produce what forms a natural set of interrelated but distinct works. Together, these three books engage the biggest societal-level issues faced by libraries: policy, inclusion, and rights and justice. This book is intended to demonstrate the interrelationships of these issues and the ways in which library activities both promote rights and justice and can serve as a means by which to promote more supportive and inclusive laws, policies, and funding decisions. The next chapter begins this exploration by detailing the path by which libraries became institutions central to human rights and social justice.

Chapter Two

The Historical Evolution of the Concepts of Human Rights and Social Justice

If you take a few moments and search the catalog of your favorite library or Amazon or some other bookseller, you will see that an impressive number of books have been written about human rights and/or social justice issues from a wide number of perspectives and from all over the world. Few of these books discuss the issues in tandem, instead inscribing themselves into one discourse or the other. More surprisingly, virtually none of them—other than the handful noted in the previous chapter—talk about libraries as part of human rights and/or social justice. And, perhaps most surprisingly, most of the books do not even discuss information or ICTs as key topics of human rights or social justice.

Human rights and social justice are both terms with heavily laden meanings. They are burdened by many tacit assumptions and preconceptions when used, and, given their enormous implications, they are among the weightiest terms in the language. There are seemingly as many uses for these terms as there are people using them. To establish the place of the arguments in this book about information and libraries within ongoing considerations of human rights and social justice, this chapter will describe the historical evolution of the interrelationship among information, human rights, and social justice.

Using the UN's UDHR and the ALA's Bill of Rights to frame the discussion, it will set forth the ways in which information access, information literacy, intellectual freedom, freedom of expression, and related principles have been increasingly recognized as central to the advancement of human rights and social justice. Focusing on the role of libraries in this evolution, this chapter also examines the library profession's involvement in issues related to human rights and social justice throughout the twentieth and twenty-first centuries. This historical overview highlights libraries' roles in providing a wide range of social services to their surrounding communities, seeking to demonstrate how libraries' commitment to access to information can also be characterized as a commitment to the advancement of human rights and social justice. This commitment, however, has been challenged by the growing acceptance of the principles of neoliberal economic and neoconservative political ideologies. The chapter concludes with a discussion of these principles to provide readers with an understanding of the tension between them and libraries' array of community roles.

A key challenge for any perspective on rights and justice is trying to understand the difficulty in implementing and protecting human rights and ensuring social justice. Though many people prefer to believe that rights are a natural part of being human, the lived human experience strongly indicates otherwise (Woodiwiss, 2005). Despite the desire by many to see human rights as a natural occurrence or as common currency among humans, the ideals of human rights are not rooted in ancient times or in a majority of cultures (Berlin, 1979; Pagels, 1979; Sellars, 2002). Considering the current and emerging roles for libraries and information within human rights and social justice, then, is a topic that is primarily confined to the past one hundred years.

THE EVOLUTION OF HUMAN RIGHTS

A number of long-standing constitutions or other kinds of founding documents contain notions of rights for at least some citizens. For example, the Magna Carta in the United Kingdom and the Declaration of Independence and Constitution of the United States include many rights that were initially intended for the moneyed and male classes of those nations. The foundation for modern conceptualizations of human rights were articulated and developed during the Enlightenment and first expressed in governance through the American and French Revolutions (Sellars, 2002). The founding documents of the United States contain both broad—and ambiguous—rights, such as the pursuit of happiness, and more specific rights to activities like assembly and expression. By no means were these documents written to create universal rights, as evidenced by the Constitution's original limitations on political participation and the inclusion of the right to keep certain types of other people as property. Despite these limitations of the founding documents, the international structures of human rights rely heavily on the Declaration of Independence in creating the notion of the state as the protector of individual rights (Calhoun, 2007). "Research on human rights consistently points to the importance of democracy in reducing the severity and incidence of personal integrity abuses" (De Mesquita, Downs, Smith, & Cherif, 2005, p. 439).

The first major proposals for what we would now think of as an international human rights structure began circulating in the 1920s as a reaction to the First World War. The modern idea of universal human rights, and what such rights might be, derives heavily from the welfare programs and social protections articulated in the United States during the Franklin Delano Roosevelt administration (Woodiwiss, 2005). The new social programs to protect the disadvantaged and ensure that basic needs were met, together with the broader ideals expressed as goals of the president, created a nascent human rights program within the United States. A speech that Roosevelt gave in 1941 advocating for an international social contract of "Four Freedoms"—to speech and expression, to religion, from want, and from fear— was a key inspiration for the development of human rights structures (Woodiwiss, 2005).

In his 1944 State of the Union address, Roosevelt used the fact that the Second World War was winding down to expand the idea of the Four Freedoms into what he hoped to be a centerpiece of his postwar legislative agenda—what he dubbed "a Second Bill of Rights" (Sunstein, 2004). He identified these new rights as including:

- A meaningful and fulfilling occupation
- A wage sufficient for adequate food, shelter, and enjoyment in life
- A decent home for every family
- An education
- A right for farms to sell their crops at a return high enough to support their farms
- A right for businesses to operate in an environment free from monopolies and unfair practices
- Adequate protection from financial uncertainty as a result of age, illness, accident, or unemployment

Proposals for an international human rights structure began circulating during and in the aftermath of World War II, such as the Conference of Evian in 1938, the Catholic Association for International Peace in 1941, and the American Law Institute's Statement of Essential Human Rights from 1946 that was directly based on Roosevelt's Four Freedoms speech (D. J. Whelan, 2010; Wronka, 1998). British author H. G. Wells even published his own idea for an international rights structure, coining the term "new world order" in the process (Sellars, 2002). From this environment of international concern for stopping future atrocities and future wars, the development of protections for human rights became a primary initial activity of the UN. The

UDHR thus represents the symbolic arrival of rights to the world stage (Raphael, 1967).

The drive to quickly establish a structure to protect human rights internationally is reflected in the fact that the UDHR was adopted in 1948 at the insistence of the U.S. government (Ignatieff, 2005). In contrast, and better reflecting the typical pace of the UN, the two accompanying covenants that elaborate on the meanings of the UDHR—the International Covenant on Civil and Political Rights and the International Covenant on Economic, Social, & Cultural Rights—were not completed until 1966. Together, these three documents are known as the International Bill of Human Rights. However, it took many subsequent years for enough countries to adopt the covenants for them to come into force (D. J. Whelan, 2010). The UDHR is now seen as customary international law (Sellars, 2002; Wronka, 1998), and internationally accepted human rights contained therein "include freedom of expression, freedom of association, freedom from fear and persecution, freedom of religion, as well as a right to shelter, education, health and work" (Halpin, Hick, & Hoskins, 2000, p. 5).

The UDHR places people as the agents of their own rights rather than the objects of rights bestowed by the nation-state (Blau & Moncada, 2006). Unlike the U.S. Constitution, which focuses on sovereignty and personal autonomy, the UDHR links individual rights with rights of community, focusing on society. The UDHR contains twenty-four specific rights. Eighteen of these rights are civil and political rights, such as expression, cultural heritage, and mobility. The remaining six are economic rights, focusing on concepts of property, employment, and social services. The UN now views these articulated human rights as being "indivisible, interdependent, and interrelated"—though none of these terms are in the UDHR—meaning that the rights must be provided and protected as a complete set (D. J. Whelan, 2010).

The UDHR and other documents have not been universally viewed as representing the interests of everyone, however. Some nations have been resistant to the UDHR on the grounds that it does not fit with what the government perceives to be the values of the national culture. Some Asian nations, as societies that historically emphasize order over individual freedom, see human rights as a threat to the community by giving too many rights to the individual (Evans, 1998). Many other nations, such as a number of former Soviet nations, have opposed human rights on nationalist grounds, where segregation and separation are more politically appealing than integration into the international community (Evans, 1998). Overall, the concept of human rights has proven more welcome in nations with a democratic government. "The significance of democracy as a way to promote respect for human rights resides in the fact that it offers the promise of providing short-term strategic guidance for reformers and policy makers" (De Mesquita et al., 2005, p. 439).

Along with certain nations rejecting the principles of the UDHR, some groups have felt excluded from the UDHR. Nonwhites, women, non-Western societies, developing nations, and the lesbian, gay, bisexual, transgender, and questioning (LGBTQ) community are among the groups that have expressed feelings of exclusion from the UDHR or a sense of disagreement with some of its underlying goals (Woodiwiss, 2005). Later conventions have been passed by the UN that have been intended to address some of these concerns, along with conventions to address issues of torture, discrimination, and the rights of children. However, the UDHR and the accompanying conventions generally have limited impact, as they "tend to be legally enforced only at the extremes of social life" (Woodiwiss, 2005, p. xv).

The UN has engaged in many further steps to encourage the adoption of and to elaborate on the International Bill of Human Rights. The 1993 Vienna World Conference on Human Rights, as one example, reaffirmed the intentional commitment to the UDHR and the subsequent conventions. Other organizations have held meetings to focus on the role of international human rights in specific areas. The 2003 and 2005 World Summits on the Information Society, for instance, yielded assertions of the importance of technology for rights to exist in the age of the Internet. However, in spite of these UN proclamations, resolutions, and summits—as well as the establishment of global and regional human rights advocates and agencies—the protection of human rights have been left primarily to national governments, local community agencies, and nongovernmental organizations (NGOs).

Ironically, after serving as a primary inspiration for and driver of the creation of an international human rights structure, the U.S. government has stepped away from a leadership role in human rights, opting not to draft or ratify many international treaties and conventions over several decades (Ignatieff, 2005). As the discourse of human rights has matured, it has emphasized certain principles that the U.S. government—particularly conservative politicians—has found likely to erode the international power of the United States or even its autonomy at home (Evans, 1998). Human rights raise these types of issues among certain groups in many nations because they are intermestic laws, meaning that they are international and national at the same time (Rosenau, 2003; Steinhardt, 1999). In the United States, exceptionalism in relation to international human rights treaties and conventions can manifest itself through official reservations about their content, denial of jurisdiction in the United States, nonratification, or noncompliance following ratification (Ignatieff, 2005).

While one certainly can have reasonable objections to specific goals of the UN, the politicians of the United States have become irrationally afraid of the UN, with conservative politicians using it as a straw man representing anything that is seen as a threat to U.S. hegemony. The bias inherent in this perceived threat is the conservative opposition to the expansion of individual rights (Moravcsik, 2005). An example of this was the recent failure of the U.S. Senate to ratify a UN convention for the protection of rights of persons with disabilities. Based entirely on existing U.S. law, this convention did not create a single new legal obligation for the U.S. government—as the United States is the undisputed international leader in crafting legal protections for people with disabilities (Jaeger, 2012, 2013)—yet the majority of senators rejected it for interfering with U.S. law. Fortunately, as the case of disability rights demonstrates, the principles of human rights created and fostered by the United States still manage to have global impact even when the United States fails to participate directly in their spread (Moravcsik, 2005).

THE EVOLUTION OF LIBRARIES AS COMMUNITY ORGANIZATIONS

Long before the language of human rights or social justice existed, however, libraries were providing services that would pave the way for their ever-expanding roles in these areas. In the 1850s, the modern movement for the creation of publically supported and publically accessible libraries in schools and communities was positioning libraries as a solution to community problems. One of the late 1800s economic arguments in favor of building libraries was that they should be viewed as "public works," as essential as a municipal water system to community health (Augst, 2007). While the level of engagement of libraries in their communities has progressed considerably over the past century—from an organization that was there to promote the reading of certain types of materials to one that provides what the community indicates that it needs—it has been a unifying notion for libraries that they exist to help the community in some fashion (Jaeger, Gorham, Bertot, & Sarin, 2014). "The information professions have long been associated with inclusiveness, civic-mindedness, and concern for the poor and underserved" (Rioux, 2010, p. 9).

Libraries began to more openly embrace and define themselves around these community service roles in the 1960s. During that decade, the term "social responsibility" became a central part of library discourse. Debates about the extent to which librarians should be politically active, advocating for change, or taking stands on political issues were widely discussed within the profession (Schuman, 1976). The topics considered under social responsibility have included literacy, feminism, race, multiculturalism, services to immigrants, children's services, freedom of speech, and intellectual freedom (MacCann, 1989). Since it was first used, social responsibility has been a contested term within librarianship, as different groups of librarians feel varying degrees of obligation to or professional appropriateness of proactively reaching out to help address community problems (Raber, 2007; Raymond, 1979). The explicit embrace of social responsibility language and action began as a reaction in the 1960s to what was seen as library leadership, particularly ALA, being too cautious.

Libraries have also evidenced a long-view commitment to "community building" or "community librarianship" or, more actively phrased as "libraries building communities." This approach includes both establishing and cultivating community partnerships and focusing on developing services for underserved groups in the community, such as immigrants, those with low literacy levels, rural populations, youth, and socioeconomically disadvantaged populations (McCook, 2000; Wilson & Birdi, 2008). The establishment of information and referral services in libraries in the early 1970s—the purpose of which was to coordinate the delivery of human services information at a community level so as to help people navigate the maze of social service programs—aptly demonstrates the role that libraries can play in community building (Poe, 2006). And, more recently, since the beginning of the Great Recession, libraries have increasingly focused on the development of partnerships with other government agencies, nonprofit organizations, and others to provide services that they cannot provide individually (Bertot & Jaeger, 2012; Gorham, Bertot, Jaeger, & Taylor, 2013; Jaeger, Taylor, Bertot, Perkins, & Wahl, 2012; N. G. Taylor, Gorham, Jaeger, & Bertot, 2014).

The commitment of libraries and librarians to promoting concepts that are now considered issues of human rights and social justice is demonstrated by the fact that the ALA's Library Bill of Rights predates the UDHR (McCook, 2011). In reaction to global events, the ALA passed its Library Bill of Rights in 1939. This time period is generally identified in library histories as the beginning of libraries viewing and labeling themselves as forces of intellectual freedom, civil rights, and democratic ideals—the proverbial marketplace of ideas (Berninghausen, 1953; Geller, 1974; Hafner, 1987; Harris, 1973, 1976; Heckart, 1991; Robbins, 1996; Smith, 1995). In the civil rights movement, for example, the ALA boycotted convention cities that were segregated, cut ties with segregated state library associations, amended the Library Bill of Rights to condemn limitations on library use based on race, and conducted studies of equity of access in the South (Cresswell, 1996). Local libraries in many places went further, with some taking a lead in the civil rights movement at the local level (Robbins, 2000, 2007). Public library "read-ins" were important to breaking down segregation not only in Southern libraries, but also in other public institutions in Southern communities (P. T. Graham, 2001). And while librarians were not typically behind the creation of Freedom Libraries in towns where public library use was segregated, such libraries were profound statements of the power of libraries in the struggle for equal rights (Cook, 2008; Selby, 2013).

While libraries have performed both civilizing and liberating functions from the beginning, the devotion to collections, services, and outreach to promote inclusion in communities and to promote the rights of individuals began in earnest in the era of the First World War (Kerslake & Kinnell, 1998). A central component of the ALA's stance is the unswerving assertion that community members must have access to a full range of perspectives on all significant political and social issues to be both informed and able to participate (Samek, 2001). Overall, many ALA policies and bodies have been created with a social justice focus, such as services to disadvantaged groups, persons with disabilities, and the poor, as well as the many associations for different service needs and populations within ALA (McCook, 2011).

Additional ALA organizational activities demonstrating this commitment to human rights and social justice can be seen in the creation of the ALA Office of Library Service to the Disadvantaged in 1970, the incorporation of the UDHR into the ALA Policy Manual in 1991, and the presence of many human rights and social justice issues in the ALA Bill of Rights, Core Values, and Policy Manual. Libraries have also been instrumental in major issues of rights and justice in their local communities, ranging from combating government censorship and protecting patron privacy to taking leadership in promoting the inclusion of many disadvantaged populations (Jaeger & Burnett, 2005; Jaeger, Gorham, Bertot, & Sarin, 2014).

As an example, the evolution of libraries into institutions focused on issues of human rights and social justice both at the local and national level can be viewed through the perspective of evolving services to immigrants (Jaeger, Gorham, Bertot, & Sarin, 2014). Library outreach and services for immigrants date back to the early years of the public library movement in the late 1800s and early 1900s (Burke, 2008; Jones, 1999). Before World War I, libraries were particularly focused on providing services to immigrant children and first-generation Americans (Larson, 2001; McDowell, 2010, 2011). A range of materials and services were provided for young patrons as individuals and in reading and social groups focusing on a range of subject matters—literature, arts, economics, politics, and employment—with a heavy emphasis on enculturation and acclimation to the United States (Larson, 2001). These services for children were also seen as a way to reach their parents and help Americanize them (McDowell, 2011). Such services were provided in a climate "indifferent and at times even hostile" to the educational needs of young immigrants and first-generation Americans (Larson, 2001, p. 225).

By the time America entered World War I, immigrant services had been widely accepted as a key function of libraries in urban areas, as the country was absorbing many more immigrants from a wider range of places than previously received (Wiegand, 1986, 1989). The ALA began programs to promote the socialization of these new waves of immigrants and assistance in the transition from immigrant to citizen through library services (Burke, 2008; Jones, 1999; Wiegand, 1986). The increasing focus on the needs of immigrants led to a stronger focus on the needs of other disadvantaged groups, playing a significant part in the maturation of the library into a progressive community institution (Jones, 1999). These occurred in conjunction with other service innovations in libraries, such as children's services, adult services, reference, tutoring, creative arts programs, practical skills programs for adults, lectures, concerts, and exhibits (Davies, 1974; DuMont, 1977). In this same time period, libraries in cities were among the first public institutions to adopt modern approaches to ventilation, lighting, and sanitation (Musman, 1993).

The Great Depression further cemented the role of libraries in meeting the broad needs of their community members. During the Great Depression, library services and materials were "eagerly sought" and "contributed something to the lessening of social ills during a difficult period" (Herdman, 1943, p. 334). The demand for library books and for reference services skyrocketed; between 1930 and 1932, circulation at libraries around the country jumped by 25 to 30 percent annually, though those averages were down to 14 percent by 1935 as libraries had fewer materials left for patrons (Herdman, 1943; Waples, Carnovsky, & Randall, 1932). The increased demand coupled with budget decreases left many libraries with decimated collections by the end of the Depression (Kramp, 1975/2010). The needs of patrons during the Depression also led to expansions of services for unemployed adults and of children's services, creating "a broader concept of community service" that continues to this day (Ennis & Fryden, 1960, p. 253). Yet, a lack of funds drove libraries to stop buying materials and hiring new employees—a whole generation of library school graduates had to take jobs without pay simply to be able to work in their chosen fields (Joeckel, 1932; Shera, 1933). In the Great Depression and subsequent periods of economic distress, the patrons of libraries would benefit greatly from many services originally created to help new immigrants (Berman, 1998; Nyquist, 1968).

Stemming from this increased focus on community needs during times of turmoil, libraries now often provide information on and services related to citizenship, employment, education, social services, health, safety, housing, and learning English, as well as materials in native languages, aiding immigrants in their acclimation to a new country (Cuban, 2007; McCook, 2011; Varheim, 2010). In many communities, the library is still the most important institution available to immigrants in adapting to their new lives and new communities, while also helping to preserve identities and connections to original cultures (Caidi & Allard, 2005; Cuban, 2007; Lukenbill, 2006; McCook, 2007; Mehra & Srinivasan, 2007). As a result of these targeted programs and services, immigrant populations typically perceive the public library as a place of building social networks, learning about their place of residence, meeting new people in the community, staying connected to their native cultures, and learning to trust social institutions, in addition to the information resources and language services available (Audunson, Essmat, & Aabo, 2011; Chu, 1999; Varheim, 2010). Inclusive services to immigrant populations is also a topic that is part of the curriculum of some library schools (Jaeger, Subramaniam, Jones, & Bertot, 2010).

The advent of the World Wide Web has provided new opportunities for public libraries to provide innovative services to immigrants. Many libraries across the country, for example, are playing a pivotal role in helping immigrants attain citizenship. Over the past several years, public libraries in several regions with high levels of immigration have partnered with other social agencies to provide wide-ranging assistance through the immigration process, with a few libraries even becoming the immigration centers for their regions (Gorham, Bertot, Jaeger, & Taylor, 2013). These long-running and recent initiatives for immigrant populations are but one example of many in which libraries have made—and continue to make—their communities far more inclusive than would otherwise be the case.

NEOCONSERVATISM AND NEOLIBERALISM

Yet, as libraries have increasingly taken on essential roles to promote human rights and social justice communities, library support—both financial and political—has been slashed at the local, state, and federal levels. In a political climate centered on cutting costs, libraries have been targeted as an unwise expenditure of public funds (Jaeger, Gorham, Bertot, & Sarin, 2014). Some jurisdictions have moved to privatize their libraries and library services; some commentators claim that Google has eliminated the need for libraries; and *Forbes* magazine continues to label an MLS as the worst master's degree to earn (Bertot, Jaeger, & Sarin, 2012). This overall denigration of the value of libraries among economic, political, and policy-making circles has accelerated since the Ronald Reagan administration in the 1980s, being driven by the widespread embrace of the principles of neoliberal economic and neoconservative political ideologies. These forces work in tandem to undermine the value accorded to public goods and public services in policy-making and political contexts by demanding that public institutions demonstrate the economic contributions of service to the public.

The neoliberal economic ideology is an approach to the economy that extends beyond economic policy, mandating that decisions of governance be based on what is best for markets. Under this approach, economic, political, and social decisions are driven by market concerns and organized by the language and rationality of markets. The neoliberal ideology is designed to support the consolidation of wealth and influence through the "creative destruction" of institutions with egalitarian objectives (Harvey, 2007a, 2007b). As such, neoliberalism is the key force in moving support away from public entities to private ones, serving to undermine the ability of many public institutions—such as libraries and schools—to meet the same goals that they were once able to (Buschman, 2012). As president, Reagan liked to frequently repeat the joke that the nine scariest words in the English language were: "I'm from the government and I'm here to help."

In 1987, after being elected prime minister for a third consecutive term, Margaret Thatcher stated: "There is no such thing as society"; instead, "the great driving engine, the driving force of life" is individuals and groups wanting to make money (Thatcher, 1987). This statement was a clear window into the thinking of adherents of neoliberalism. Without society, nothing can be the fault of society, alleviating government of the need to look after members of society who are in need of help. Without the need to support members of a society, institutions of the public good become utterly superfluous. Now, there are at least three different major arguments that society does not exist, all emanating from the neoliberal economic ideology and being united by a central premise that rejects any central structure binding people together beyond economics (Dean, 2013). The past several decades have provided numerous other examples of this approach, with many attempts to transform previously common functions of society into ones of self-care, using the language of consumerism to do so. A famous example of this was President George W. Bush's ultimately unsuccessful proposal to change Social Security to individual retirement accounts, under which citizens would have been left to fend for themselves in the market.

The movement to require all government functions to justify themselves in economic terms may be the essence of the neoliberal economic ideology, with many public goods being assessed as cost calculations. Al Gore spent much of his eight years as Bill Clinton's vice president spearheading efforts throughout government—known collectively as National Performance Review studies—to focus on efficiency, productivity, and profitability rather than good governance or the public good. A little-remembered part of the early development of e-government was that Gore initially advocated for it as a revenue stream for government, which would have forced citizens to pay for searches, transactions, and interactions with government that they would only be able to do online. Ultimately, the notion that all government functions can and should have a clear economic value has led to dwindling investments in and support of education, physical infrastructure, benefits, workplace safety, environmental safety, and libraries, among many other government functions.

Neoliberalism has become the driver of "policy and economic discussions," but it also "has a strong and fluid cultural aspect" (Buschman, 2012,

p. 9). Thus, as the neoliberal economic ideology has greatly decreased regulation of the corporation, the moralistic aspect of the neoconservative political ideology has increased the regulation of the citizen. The neoconservative political ideology is based on the idea that the state should exercise power as moral authority rather than through representative governance. A neoconservative state is strong and willing to use that strength to accomplish policy goals that may be driven entirely by moral evaluations, such as "wars of choice." Limitations on previously established rights, such as limiting women's access to the services of reproductive choice as a way to curtail the ability to seek an abortion, amount to moralistic regulations on citizens. The moral basis of governance is embraced by the elected officials who embrace the neoconservative ideology. President George W. Bush famously spoke of his decisions in terms of "political capital" that he had earned and could spend as he saw fit, rather than in terms of trying to represent the interests and perspectives of the governed.

Neoconservatism also belittles educational institutions, like schools and libraries, as serving to erode the values of the supposed majority. The field of education was far more attuned to the ways in which neoconservatives were framing education than the field of librarianship, with assessments of the impact of neoconservatives already appearing in education discourse before Reagan was elected (Park, 1980). Libraries certainly did everything they possibly could to reinforce the narrative in the minds of neoconservatives—and much of the general public—that they were actively threatening community values based on the way ALA's challenges to CIPA played out in the courts.

Under the combination of the neoconservative and neoliberal ideologies, the rights of corporations prevail over the rights of both individuals and educational institutions. When failed Republican presidential nominee Mitt Romney stated, "Corporations are people, too" in a 2012 campaign speech, it was no mistake. Corporations are also much more likely than individuals to garner political support and funding for the infrastructure on which they depend—roads, railways, shipping, and power and other utilities—and the government generally acts to ensure that those corporate infrastructure needs are met.

Since the combination of these ideologies swept into common usage under the Reagan and Thatcher administrations in the United States and the United Kingdom, respectively, the result has been radical change through reductions in tax rates, spending cuts for public services, deregulation, and erosions of social support for the public good. In a public discourse in which every public good can be questioned and required to demonstrate a tangible value, economic terminology began to dominate public discourse. Yet, economics and economic analysts are not neutral. By treating political and moral questions as being interchangeable with economic ones, these ideologies have allowed for political discourse and policy-making processes to question anything to which it is hard to assign a tangible value or that does not comply with a strict moral vision of the government. Being a public good is no longer sufficient to warrant support.

The omnipresence of these ideologies at the federal level has resulted in their widespread adoption in lower levels of government as well. Unfortunately, the market and the government provide services in very different ways. Public goods can deliver many kinds of contributions, supporting democratic equality, social efficiency, and social mobility (Labaree, 1997). However, because many elements of the public good are not easy to monetize, decreasing government support to them will not easily be replaced by support from the market. Human rights and social justice, unfortunately, are not especially profitable from the perspective of economics or markets.

In the recent years of the prolonged global economic downturn, the emphasis on the devaluing of public services has been extended under the buzzword of "austerity." While clearly an intentionally ambiguous term, austerity provides a means to justify deeper cuts into public goods and services that cannot articulate an economically quantified value and/or that are deemed morally objectionable under the neoconservative ideology. As the language of value is based on economic contributions rather than public good, the terms of austerity are clearly biased against educational and cultural institutions like libraries. By targeting institutions such as libraries, austerity policies ironically serve to undermine the only institutions that exist to provide the digital literacy skills and education necessary for many people to be able to participate in the workforce. As will be explored in the next chapter, these digital literacy and digital inclusion activities by libraries are among their most significant contributions to their communities and are a central part of their human rights and social justice roles.

Chapter Three

The Current State of Digital Inclusion

As the Internet facilitates access to information that is a necessary part of everyday life, access to the Internet itself and the ability to use it now can (and should) be characterized as a human right. The following section of the 2011 General Comment to the United Nations International Covenant on Civil and Political Rights makes the connection between technology and equality clear, by making governments responsible for promoting new technologies:

> States parties should take account of the extent to which developments in information and communication technologies, such as internet and mobile based electronic information dissemination systems, have substantially changed communication practices around the world. There is now a global network for exchanging ideas and opinions that does not necessarily rely on the traditional mass media intermediaries. States parties should take all necessary steps to foster the independence of these new media and to ensure access of individuals thereto. (UN, 2011)

The *level* of access available to the Internet is also important. Full digital inclusion, or "access to the Internet in order to apply the skills of digital literacy" (Thompson et al., 2014, p. 1) is essential for such diverse life needs as job applications, government service requests, e-commerce, and education. The requirements of this technology include digital literacy, or "the ability to use the Internet to meet information needs" (Thompson et al., 2014, p. 1). Traditionally, U.S. policies have considered access as the ability to physically reach technology, particularly having broadband access, owning a computer, or being able to purchase affordable Internet plans. However, as explained in chapter 1, this book defines access more broadly, along the lines of physical, social, and intellectual access. The tension between these narrow

and broad conceptualizations can be seen in the access gaps created by legislation passed in the United States and the ongoing struggle of libraries to fill
these gaps.

To explore this further, this chapter will discuss the approaches that the
U.S. government has taken to digital inclusion through policies, laws, regulations, and other instruments of government. Then, an overview of gaps in
access that have been created by these government instruments will be discussed, as well as the ways in which these gaps affect populations differently, in many cases exacerbating existing social injustices. Finally, the chapter
will explore the ways that libraries strive to close these gaps in access. First,
though, this chapter will explore the language of digital inclusion, focusing
on the definition of the term "digital divide" in policy and academic rhetoric.

DEFINING THE DIGITAL DIVIDE

As mentioned, digital inclusion has frequently been conceptualized in terms
of physical access. This idea has been prevalent since the Internet was introduced to the masses in the mid-1990s. Because prices for online connections
and hardware were so high, many in scholarly communities and public service began to fear that populations who already lacked ready access to information would be even further shut out of discourse. Potter (2006) describes
"zones of silence" to describe "the unseen, seemingly quiet, technology-
sparse spaces of the digital divide" and those who are cut off from widespread communication networks. In academic and policy circles, this concern
became known as the *digital divide* (Barber, 1997; De Cindio, Gentile, Grew,
& Redolfi, 2003; Nicholas, 2003; Norris, 2001; O'Neil & Baker, 2003;
Sawhney, 2003; Servon, 2002; Stanley, 2003; Strover, 2003; Thompson,
2008; van Dijk & Hacker, 2003; Warschauer, 2003; Wresch, 1996).

Early researchers of this phenomenon mirrored authors of poverty literature in that they examined factors leading to poverty from a noneconomic
view. As discussed in Thompson et al. (2014), these factors included gender
(Nath, 2001), geographic location (Bertot & McClure, 1999; Jue, Koontz,
Magpantay, Lance, & Seidl, 1999; Nicholas, 2003), community networks or
barriers (De Cindio et al., 2003; Gurstein, 2003; O'Neil & Baker, 2003),
disability (First & Hart, 2002; Jaeger, 2012), social factors (Burnett & Jaeger, 2012; Jaeger & Thompson, 2003, 2004; Mathiesen, 2014a; Oltmann,
2009; Thompson, 2008; Thompson & Afzal, 2011), education level (Hendry,
2000; National Telecommunications and Information Administration
[NTIA], 1999), psychosocial barriers to information (Stanley, 2003), and
income (Warschauer, 2003). At the same time, policy documents (and admit-
tedly many scholarly studies as well) considered the digital divide a binary
phenomenon—people either had access to technology or they did not; they

used technology or they did not; they understood technology or they did not. The series of NTIA reports in the 1990s and early 2000s demonstrate this perspective (NTIA, 1995, 1998, 1999, 2000, 2002).

As the Internet was diffused into everyday life, it became obvious that just owning a technology device was not enough to guarantee understanding or use. The binary view of "haves" and "have-nots" ignores the fact that people use technology for different reasons (Bertot, 2003). Not every population will find content equally meaningful, and some may find content irrelevant, in spite of its actual applicability (Selwyn, Gorard, & Furlong, 2005). In addition, as this book makes clear by the use of the tripartite access model, users need a variety of skills, literacies, and social support to adequately use technology. Hargittai and Walejko (2008) note the emergence of a participation gap among young people, in which those from lower socioeconomic backgrounds have different relationships to content on the Internet than other populations.

Interestingly, the concept of the digital divide is not often discussed in books specifically about human rights and social justice, and when it is discussed, the focus is less practical and more as part of larger societal injustices (Greenstein & Esterhuysen, 2012; Roth, 2000). While this is an important part of technology access gaps, and one that has been acknowledged by many scholars (Servon, 2002; Stevenson, 2009), it is curious that the concept is not more prevalent in work focused on human rights and social justice.

Though the view of the digital divide as one of "have" and "have-nots" has become less prevalent in recent years, both in government and non-government reports (Fink & Kenny, 2003; Horrigan & Rainie, 2002a, 2002b; Kommers & Rainie, 2002; Larsen & Rainie, 2002; Mossberger, Tolbert, & McNeal, 2008; Mossberger, Tolbert, & Stansbury, 2003; Strover, 2003; van Dijk & Hacker, 2003), the influence of the binary conceptualization of the digital divide still permeates policy decisions. To see this influence, it is instructive to look at the U.S. policies that focus on digital inclusion issues.

U.S. LEGISLATION RELATED TO DIGITAL INCLUSION

There are three seminal acts of legislation that lay the groundwork for digital inclusion policies in the United States; each one, of course, has spawned a variety of other policies, which are discussed below. The first, the Communications Act of 1934, established standards to promote equity of access to wire and radio communication technology. Although created before widespread adoption of digital technology was a possibility, the act placed the federal government as the arbiter of ensuring that telecommunications should be nondiscriminatory and affordable to all.

The most recent major update to this law was the Telecommunications Act of 1996, which continued to emphasize inclusion in its policy rhetoric. The Telecommunications Act, developed alongside the Clinton administration's focus on the country's widely variable access to the Internet, stressed the need for affordable access to telephone lines (the primary means of access to the Internet at the time), and, unlike the 1934 legislation, provided mechanisms for funding assistance programs. The most robust of these programs was the Universal Service Fund (USF), through which the education rate (E-rate) funding program was established. The Federal Communications Commission (FCC) has provided billions of dollars in financial aid for Internet connectivity in rural health-care providers, almost all public schools, and about 50 percent of public libraries through the USF and E-rate program (Jaeger, Bertot, McClure, & Rodriguez, 2007; Jaeger, McClure, & Bertot, 2005; Jaeger & Yan, 2009). The 1990s also saw the creation of the Link-Up America program and the Lifeline Assistance program. These programs were designed to assist low-income Americans with both installation and monthly bills associated with telecommunications services.

Most recently, the American Reinvestment and Recovery Act (ARRA) has continued the theme of financial assistance for equal access to telecommunications. ARRA provided $7.2 billion in funding for loans and grants to be offered and administered by the NTIA and the U.S. Department of Agriculture's Rural Utilities Service (RUS). The majority of the funding ($4.7 billion) was to be used to build broadband infrastructure in underserved and unserved areas, with $2.5 billion specifically for rural areas (White House, 2009). ARRA established the Broadband Technology Opportunities Program (BTOP) to provide grants to both increase broadband access and inclusion. Through BTOP, NTIA awarded grants in three categories: (1) deployment of broadband infrastructure; (2) creation and expansion of public computer centers; and (3) the promotion of sustainable adoption of broadband services. The program also funded the gathering of state data "on the availability, speed, and location of broadband services, as well as the broadband services that community institutions, such as schools, libraries and hospitals, use" (NTIA, n.d.). This data was collected and, in collaboration with the FCC, was used to develop the National Broadband Map in 2011 (http:// broadbandmap.gov). The Broadband Initiatives Program (BIP) was also developed with ARRA funds. Operated by RUS, the funds (primarily loans) were devoted to projects that provided access to customers (285 last-mile projects), transmissions lines for large areas (twelve middle-mile awards), and satellite and technical assistance awards (four and nineteen, respectively). This funding was distributed among forty-five states and one territory (Department of Agriculture, 2011).

In 2010, as required by ARRA, the FCC released the National Broadband Plan, consisting of recommendations to "guide the path forward through the rulemaking process at the FCC, in Congress and across the Executive Branch" (FCC, 2010, p. ix). In an effort to consolidate and improve broadband policy, the FCC's plan attempts to address the issue of broadband availability through a variety of issues, including development, the economic market, and the reform and creation of policies. The plan conceptualizes digital inclusion as adequate and affordable broadband service and the means to develop digital literacy needed to use broadband effectively. To promote inclusion, the FCC suggests the use of incentives. The plan, for example, proposes the transfer of USF investments to a new Connect America Fund as a means to promote the expansion of broadband access (FCC, 2010).

These policies, while seemingly well intentioned, all share three limitations that have major impacts on their usefulness in addressing inequalities. First, as mentioned above, these policies tend to favor a conceptualization of the digital divide that places emphasis on physical access. One example of this is the FCC's creation of community technology centers (CTCs), established after the passage of the 1996 Telecommunications Act. CTCs were intended to create spaces where people could access hardware outside of their homes, but failed due to a lack of consideration for the need for digital literacy training and social trust, both of which could be, and already were, found in libraries (Jaeger & Fleischmann, 2007). This emphasis on physical access is also evident in the distribution of BTOP grants. Of the $4 billion NTIA invested in 233 BTOP projects, the majority of these funds—$3.5 billion for 123 infrastructure projects—went toward the construction of broadband networks (NTIA, 2014). This focus on physical access also extends beyond the borders of the United States. In 2012, the UN's Broadband Commission for Digital Development—overseen by the International Telecommunication Union (ITU)—vowed to "boost the importance of broadband on the international policy agenda" by focusing on infrastructure and network issues (Broadband Commission for Digital Development, n.d.).

One of the more striking recent examples is the July 2014 FCC order to modernize the E-rate program to focus on more general broadband connectivity and to expand Wi-Fi networks in schools and libraries. The order established goals to: "Significantly expand funding for Wi-Fi networks and distribute it fairly to all schools and libraries while recognizing the needs of the nation's rural and poorest school districts; maximize the cost-effectiveness of E-rate spending through greater pricing transparency, encouraging consortia and bulk purchasing, and better enforcement of existing rules; [and] streamline and simplify the E-rate application process and overall program administration" (FCC, 2014a). In theory, Wi-Fi access is of growing importance to schools and libraries, making this a smart allocation of resources. In practice, congressional critics of the plan pointed to the potential for limiting traditional access. In a letter to FCC chairman Thomas Wheeler, Senators Rockefeller and Markey wrote that "it would be ill-advised to guarantee a permanent set-aside for Wi-Fi, if that set-aside could end up cannibalizing funding for basic Internet connectivity" (Rockefeller & Markey, 2014 , p. 2). In addition, some suggested that "Wheeler's proposal to limit subsidy allocation on a per-pupil level would severely disadvantage smaller, poorer and rural schools" (Baschuk, 2014, n.p.). Finally, many were concerned with the fact that the new order does not eliminate the annual budget cap for E-rate expenditures (Baschuk, 2014). This could eventually create enormous deficits of affordable access in the very public spaces that people turn to for digital literacy training and public Internet access. In December 2014, the FCC adopted a second E-rate modernization order focusing on, among other things, closing the gap between rural and urban schools, as well as approving a $1.5 billion funding increase for the program (FCC, 2014b). The outcome of implementation remains to be seen, and critics will likely continue to decry the funding.

Second, though the rhetoric of the policies is promising, their implementations and outcomes display the underlying political and economic influences of neoliberalism (discussed in chapter 2), which operate to limit the government's concern with equity to information, social justice, or human rights. "The neoliberal economic ideology . . . extends beyond economic policy, mandating that decisions of governance be based on what is best for markets, as free markets are seen as being dependent on all decisions reinforcing their freedom" (Jaeger, Gorham, Bertot, & Sarin, 2014, p. 63). The language used in scholarly and policy discussions of the new "information age" reflect this ideology as well:

> The term "knowledge economy" implies the commodification of knowledge, a process that transforms experience and information into marketable products and services. Access to these products and services is then supposed to be regulated by the law of demand and supply. This trend might result in more widespread distribution of knowledge and information, but it is also likely to result in restricted access for those without the resources needed to buy their way into this economy. (Greenstein & Esterhuysen, 2012, p. 282)

As Roth (2000) asks, "Within the Internet world's emerging structures, dominant qualities, values and principles underlying North/West societies—a market economy and corporatist ethic and aesthetic . . . information as commodity; notions of citizens as consumers, among others—are subtly embedded. . . . Why should we expect Internet institutional systems, structures, sites, services, and access and user politics to be any different from those evident in the societies from which they emerge?" (p. 177).

As public institutions existing in this new economy over the last two decades, both public schools and public libraries have been called upon to demonstrate a clear economic value. These two public institutions, however, have responded in very different ways. Public schools have worked to define value on their own terms, relying on teacher evaluations, standardized testing, and similar metrics. Because libraries are not able to perform assessment tests on patrons to determine how much they have learned from the library or how well they fit predetermined metrics for achievement, they have often drawn from business and economic perspectives, relying on metrics such as return on investment (ROI) to demonstrate value. The ALA even promotes a "Library Value Calculator" to calculate how much money a library system is saving its community. As will be discussed in chapter 6, this approach has also led some within the library community to consider different models of privatization (Streitfeld, 2010). School libraries, operating at the nexus of public schools and library ideals, continue to struggle with defining value in these ways, perhaps leading to the deep cuts in personnel and funding over the past few years (ALA, 2013c).

Finally, there are political realities that exist as a result of the United States' fragmented political system that hinder digital inclusion efforts. Elected government officials overseeing agencies in charge of policy implementation generally have exceedingly short attention spans. The 2002 NTIA study entitled *A Nation Online: How Americans Are Expanding Their Use of the Internet* marked a significant departure from the previous focus on "Falling Through the Net." The shift from discussing groups in the United States who still lacked Internet access to celebrating the progress made in this area reveals a keen desire to show clear success, thus allowing the government to move on to other issues. DigitalLiteracy.gov is another example; created by a team of federal agencies at the behest of the Obama administration, the site aims to "serve as a valuable resource to practitioners who are delivering digital literacy training and services in their communities" (DigitalLiteracy.gov, n.d.). The site fails, however, to offer continued interaction with intermediaries, as evidenced by the limited number of responses to comments and questions on posts.

Inclusion and literacy are long-term goals. Work toward equality is never finished, especially as technology continues to evolve. True commitment to these goals requires a much stronger emphasis on long-term funding for evaluation of programs and limits the false claims of completion commonly desired in political rhetoric. In the FCC's National Broadband Plan, affordable and adequate broadband services, as well as digital literacy education, are all emphasized. The language of the report makes it clear, however, that the FCC recognizes the loftiness of these goals, as well as its own lack of enforcement ability. These recommendations are offered as suggestions ("should") rather than requirements ("must"), which fails to inspire much confidence in the actual realization of these ideals.

DIGITAL EXCLUSION — OR FAILURES OF LEGISLATION

The government's lack of steadfast attention to digital inclusion issues has led to the perpetuation of gaps in access, many of which can be traced to traditional definitions of information poverty and often exacerbating existing social injustices. Though information poverty can be viewed through many lenses (Branscomb, 1979; Buckley, 1987; Childers & Post, 1975; Coleman, 1972; Companie, 1986; Dhillon, 1980; Dubey,1985; Duran, 1978; Gannett Center for Media Studies, 1987; Greenberg & Dervin, 1970a, 1970b; Lang, 1988; Lewis, 1959, 1961; Mason, 1986; McClure, 1974; Menou, 1983; Murdock & Golding, 1989; Orman, 1987; E. B. Parker & Dunn, 1972; Scherer, 1989; Zukin & Snyder, 1984), the degree to which digital technology is available is a common thread throughout modern conceptualizations. The idea of the "diffusion of innovation" (Rogers, 1995), first theorized in the 1960s, demonstrates that those with greater material wealth adopt technology earlier than those with less income, allowing them to get the earliest and greatest benefits from the technology.

Indeed, the distribution of hardware and Internet connectivity hinges on many levels of access, including affordability. The Great Recession has prompted many to turn to the library as home Internet access becomes a budgetary luxury for many individuals and families (Bertot, 2009; Bertot, Jaeger, McClure, Wright, & Jensen, 2009; Jaeger & Bertot, 2010, 2011; Powell, Byrne, & Dailey, 2010). Library data shows that, in 2009, approximately three-fourths of libraries reported increased usage of both workstations and wireless usage over the previous year (ALA, 2010b). The fact that libraries experience such increases in patronage during times of economic downturns is so predictable that it has been coined the *librarian's axiom* (Davis, 2009, 2011; James, 1986; Lynch, 2002).

Making matters more complicated, the evolution of technology is such that mere access to Internet technology is no longer enough. With the advent of Web 2.0 and its accompanying social media, audio, and video sharing, bandwidth is increasingly important to meaningful access. There is a direct correlation between income level and home broadband access; whereas 85 percent of Americans earning over $100,000 per year have home broadband access, only 25 percent of Americans earning less than $25,000 per year have home broadband access (Horrigan, 2009).

Gaps in access are not solely due to wealth. As a series of Pew Internet & the American Life reports have shown, language and education are both tied to use of the Internet. Non-English speakers are at a particular disadvantage; the difference in use of the Internet between Latinos in the United States who do not speak English and those who do is more than 45 percent (32 percent as compared to 78 percent) (Fox & Livingston, 2007; Livingston, 2010). Formal education is also a factor in digital access (Jaeger & Thompson, 2003,

2004; Powell, Byrne, & Dailey, 2010). Ultimately, digital literacy involves a wide range of skills, including the ability to:

> identify, find, retrieve, and manage digital information in various formats. For one to be able to access digital information . . . to integrate, evaluate, analyze, and synthesize digital information and construct new knowledge based on the information found . . . to develop a personal information strategy, develop questions that will solve information and knowledge needs, use relevant information to solve the information problem at hand, and protect his or her privacy and confidentiality while seeking, retrieving, and sharing information . . . [and] to communicate digital information with others, determine constructive social actions based on the information received, and reflect upon this process. (Thompson et al., 2014, p. 52)

Thus, teaching someone with little formal education or training to be able to adequately access the Internet is not as simple as pointing that individual to an instructional brochure or website. Additionally, people with disabilities face tremendous barriers to use of the Internet, including lack of affordable hardware, inaccessible Internet service providers (ISPs), and incompatibility of software with assistive technologies (Fox, 2004; Fox & Madden, 2005; Jaeger & Bowman, 2005; University of California, Los Angeles, 2003). For these reasons, the percentages of people with disabilities in the United States who use the Internet are staggeringly low as compared to the rest of the population—less than half in terms of owning a computer at home, having household access, home use, and use outside the home (Dobransky & Hargittai, 2006; Jaeger, 2012).

These statistics make it obvious that there are inequalities along each of the physical, intellectual, and social dimensions of access. Because of the enormous influence of these technologies on modern society, it is impossible to consider human rights and social justice related to information without considering digital inclusion efforts. Despite the fair amount of attention the federal government has given to issues of digital literacy and digital inclusion over the past two decades, these policies—as implemented—have yet to adequately address the full range of access issues inherent in the right to information.

LIBRARIES AND DIGITAL INCLUSION

Ultimately, libraries may be the only institutions capable of filling the gaps in physical, intellectual, and social access created by existing digital literacy and digital inclusion policies. While libraries historically have encouraged free and open access to information (as discussed in chapter 2), their role in assisting users with new technology is increasingly becoming the largest part of their services to their communities. Close to 100 percent of public libraries in the United States offer general computer skills, training in general computer software use, and training in general Internet use (Bertot, Jaeger, et al., 2014). In addition, almost all public libraries offer assistance in filling out online government forms, nearly three-fourths of libraries assist patrons with employment databases, and close to 60 percent help patrons use online business information resources (Bertot, Jaeger, et al., 2014). School and academic libraries also aim to teach digital literacy skills. School librarians incorporate integrated technology into school curriculum, including use of Web 2.0, and increasingly act as technology-focused professional development leaders for teachers in their schools. Academic librarians link information and digital literacy in student programming and partner with colleagues across their campuses (Digital Literacy Task Force, 2013).

In terms of physical access, libraries not only provide hardware and broadband access, they also frequently provide assistive technology, including screen readers, large-print book collections, audiobooks, and more. These services enable patrons with disabilities to use materials otherwise inaccessible to them. Universal design for learning is increasingly a central goal of school libraries as well, leading to the development of accessible spaces and materials for students (Blue & Pace, 2011; Subramaniam, Oxley, & Kodama, 2013).

The homeless population, often barred from other social institutions, frequently finds refuge in public libraries, gaining both physical and social access. Some public libraries, such as those in San Francisco, have dedicated programs for this population, including social workers with offices in the libraries. Immigrants, already discussed in chapter 2, also frequently find services in the public library when they have no other place to turn.

In addition, libraries are often the institutions to which the government turns when policies and means of information distribution require intermediaries to help citizens to access information. Libraries have frequently been called upon to encourage and train their communities to use digital resources. The switch to online applications for Medicare Part D in the early 2000s is an early example of this phenomenon. Libraries were flooded with patrons, many of whom had never used a computer before, looking for assistance with the online form (Jaeger, 2008). More recently, efforts by the United States Citizenship and Immigration Services to streamline the immigration and naturalization processes by establishing online application procedures led to similar results in libraries across the country, with the added complication of language and cultural knowledge gaps (Gorham, Bertot, Jaeger, & Taylor, 2013).

The Affordable Care Act (ACA) provides yet another example—prior to the enrollment period in 2013, it was predicted that many of the seven million people anticipated to sign up online for health insurance would depend on public library resources and services to do so (Eberhart, 2013). Public libraries were expected to facilitate the implementation of this law by providing information to people about options and helping them enroll. Yet, as Institute of Museum and Library Services (IMLS) director Susan Hildreth noted, "There are no federal funds to support" libraries in these efforts (Eberhart, 2013). The end result was great differences between what libraries were able to provide to assist their patrons in signing up for health care under the ACA (Bossaller, in press; Real, McDermott, Bertot, & Jaeger, in press).

Unfortunately, as these examples demonstrate, libraries often are not given the financial and political support to carry out these goals, nor are they always acknowledged in wider policy decisions relating to information access and digital inclusion. As history has shown, "decisions about funding and other forms of support for institutions that provide the access, assistance, and education to ensure digital literacy and digital inclusion—such as public libraries, public schools, school libraries, and academic libraries—are inextricably linked to . . . sways in policy guidelines" (Thompson et al., 2014, p. 2). The United States' dominant political ideology, together with these political realities, offer an explanation as to why libraries are typically excluded from the creation and implementation of policies related to information and telecommunications. Libraries embrace social and intellectual access as goals. As these goals do not readily lend themselves to evaluation in the manner that physical access data does, libraries struggle to show the tremendous contributions libraries make to digital inclusion efforts. In addition, libraries are inherently anti-neoliberal. Though the availability of library resources, services, and programs may result in a more educated public capable of contributing to the economic livelihood of this country, the immediate cost-benefit analysis of libraries will not show this correlation. This type of economic measurement applied to amorphous public goods is almost always impossible. In addition, libraries have traditionally attempted to remain above issues of policy and politics—failing to reach out to candidates or officials to advocate for their contributions. This makes it incredibly hard to compete with special interest groups contributing millions of dollars to advocacy and lobbying efforts. ALA's Washington Office aside, the profession is hardly one known for its successful involvement in debates of policy or politics, as later chapters will discuss.

The exclusion of libraries from these policy-making processes, however, is troubling. Libraries are the information institutions most directly involved with the people who are the intended beneficiaries of these policies. Regardless of the government's commitment to digital inclusion policies, when patrons arrive at the library with the expectation of finding assistance, librarians must acknowledge them. This responsibility gives a sense of permanence to the field's attention to these issues and stands in stark contrast to the government's often fleeting interest.

INFORMATION AND THE INTERNET AS ISSUES OF HUMAN RIGHTS AND SOCIAL JUSTICE

These roles of libraries in human rights and social justice activities within their communities have been recognized within several UN documents and joint statements with library organizations. UNESCO's Universal Declaration on Cultural Diversity (2001) emphasizes free flow of information and expression as central to cultural diversity, while IFLA/UNESCO's Public Library Manifesto (1994) calls public libraries "a living force for education, culture and information." Similar language appears in the later School Library Manifesto, and IFLA/UNESCO's subsequent Multicultural Library Manifesto (2008) reinforces the connection, describing libraries as "learning, cultural, and information centres." What none of these documents do, however, is identify libraries as central to human rights and social justice, and part of the reason is that information access and use is not widely recognized as an explicit human right.

There are many relationships between information, human rights, and social justice. Within the context of rights and justice, however, information is usually broken down to a focus on specific issues, primarily access, privacy, censorship, speech, and connecting and empowering communities (Halpin, Hick, & Hoskins, 2000). In rights and justice discourse, information—especially in the context of the Internet—is seen as a positive tool to better connect people, as a negative tool to suppress and abuse people, and as a tool for promotion of the human rights movement itself. There is no assurance that good will come of making new ICTs available, rather, the "good" depends on ownership, content, access, and available connections (Hornick, 2012; Lazer, 2012). Additionally, while the Internet can increase global awareness of human rights violations, restrictions to access and expression can limit the power of the Internet as a human rights tool (Drake & Jorgensen, 2006). And, just as there have been expressions that the overall UDHR is not sufficiently inclusive and representative of views around the world, some have argued that the information-specific aspects of the UDHR are not sufficiently inclusive and representative. Article 19, which articulates the right to expression, raises concerns for people in developing countries, as many of them lack the ability to use printed/electronic sources due to factors such as no access and the dominance of oral cultures in which printed materials are not used (Raseroka, 2006).

Information and the Internet can now be seen as being central to human rights—the ability to obtain, communicate, and disseminate information is necessary for many human rights to be possible (Halpin, Hick, & Hoskins, 2000). A leading scholar of human rights recently identified one of the most significant challenges to human rights as "equal access to information and communication" (Woodiwiss, 2005, p. 121). Another scholar has labeled information as "the linchpin right" that holds the others together, particularly in online contexts (Mathiesen, 2012, 2013, 2014b). The intersection of rights, justice, and information includes issues of expression, access, privacy, intellectual property, participation, assembly, race, gender, and orientation, among others (Jorgensen, 2006a). Among the principles of the UDHR, issues of privacy, nondiscrimination, due process, education, access to public services, mobility, work, development, peace, and women's rights are all affected by the relationships of rights, justice, and information.

In short, "human rights remain unattainable in the absence of free and equitable access to reliable information. . . . When individuals and communities are denied information, it becomes much easier to exploit and suppress them" (Hussain, 2000, p. x). Starting in the 1990s, many nations have adopted "right to information" laws in recognition of the importance of information to so much of daily life (Banisar, 2006). And, yet, movements to make a right to information an explicit international human right have not succeeded.

Curiously, these movements have been strongly opposed by many international human rights groups and governments (Drake & Jorgensen, 2006). The primary argument against creating a new right is that the right to expression in Article 19 of the UDHR already covers all information issues. However, expression and access are highly debated in international circles (Jorgensen, 2006b). To interpret expression as including the range of information issues and behavior—from access, use, and exchange to literacy and inclusion—requires a much broader sense of expression than has previously been established.

The failure of the international human rights structure to officially recognize a right to information raises many serious concerns, and not just for the roles played by libraries. Consider the following issues that challenge the idea that a right to expression encompasses all information issues:

- Literacy: the ability to understand not just what a source says, but whether it is a reliable and accurate source of information (Thompson et al., 2014)
- Technological change: the existing texts of human rights cannot keep up with technological change and its implications for rights (Hamelink, 1994)
- Privilege: users can take technology so for granted that they fail to recognize others' lack of access or the massive, unseen infrastructure necessary to support their own technology usage (Mackenzie, 2010)
- Infrastructure: transnational public-private partnerships have been established to advance human rights through economic projects, such as the construction of infrastructure, particularly telecommunications infrastructure (Likosky, 2006)
- People/technology: Internet technology is now such that it can blur the lines between people and technology to the extent of turning individuals

into part of the technology, such as the "Homeless Hotspots" program that turned homeless individuals into wireless hotspots (Koepfler, Mascaro, & Jaeger, 2014)
- Influence: the readership of material online does not necessarily correlate to its influence; if something has a few readers but they are very powerful, the influence can be extensive (Hornick, 2012)

These examples are a small number of the unique challenges that information raises for existing rights and justice approaches, and all present strong reasons for the creation of explicit protections related to information and its myriad impacts.

Human rights concepts were previously tied to clear cases of "the defense of individuals against the oppression of an unjust state" (Moyn, 2012, n.p.). Now, however, the role of information is so pervasive that it is central not just to protections from state action, but is integral to individual rights to education, employment, mobility, participation, and much else.

HUMAN RIGHTS AND SOCIAL JUSTICE FROM THE LIBRARY PERSPECTIVE

Sadly but not surprisingly, in the same way that information is neglected in the international discourse about human rights and social justice, the roles of libraries in using information, education, and social services to promote human rights and social justice are downplayed. Libraries directly contribute to all of the intersections of rights, justice, and information detailed above. Yet, in the twelve chapters of the book *Human Rights in the Global Information Society* (Jorgensen, 2006a), only one chapter mentions the contributions of libraries. Part of this lack of recognition is likely tied to the fact that librarianship incorporates human rights concepts without employing the language of human rights (McCook, 2011). Another issue for libraries is that the library community has leaders, primarily organizations such as IFLA and ALA, but does not have enforcers to ensure that rights and justice activities are occurring in all libraries (Samek, 2007).

Regardless of terminology or leadership, considerations of rights and justice are primary drivers of the contributions of libraries to individuals and communities. Many of these commitments to rights and justice are long standing, if not definitional, to the profession. For example, the issue of protecting the intellectual freedom of patrons is a recurring rights and justice issue for libraries across many generations at this point in time. In the 1950s, libraries strongly resisted Cold War efforts by government agencies to learn what people were reading in libraries (B. S. Johnson, 1989). In the 1960s, libraries resisted Federal Bureau of Investigation (FBI) efforts to find out the reading habits of anti–Vietnam War protestors (Kennedy, 1989). In the 1970s and 1980s, the FBI's Library Awareness Program (LAP) again tried to gain access to patron records, and libraries once again resisted (Matz, 2008). As will be discussed in chapter 6, the post-9/11 antiterrorism laws produced another round of contention between librarians seeking to promote intellectual freedom and government agencies seeking to gather information about patrons (Jaeger, Bertot, & McClure, 2003; Jaeger, McClure, Bertot, & Snead, 2004). These are some prominent examples among a great many where librarians have emphasized issues of rights and justice above what was politically popular or politically expedient (Jaeger & Burnett, 2005). Librarians have not only succeeded in preserving and promoting intellectual freedom in these cases but, by 1990, had also convinced all but two state governments to adopt laws protecting patron privacy in libraries (Garoogian, 1991).

Human rights have been described as "the lodestar" that guides library service in the twenty-first century (McCook, 2011, p. 339). Libraries are facilitators of rights and justice because they focus on the impact of information issues on people—equality of access, information for building communities, and locally useful knowledge (Mchombu, 2004). Some librarians even believe that specific types of libraries have a more publicly clear connection to human rights than others (Bell, 2006). An example of this is public libraries across the United States providing free access to the Internet, as well as the digital literacy and inclusion to effectively use the Internet—all of which are services that embody many of the central goals of human rights (Mandel, Bishop, McClure, Bertot, & Jaeger, 2010).

The same holds true with social justice. For many librarians, being advocates and activists for rights and justice issues related to information are the reasons that they became librarians (Samek, 2007). Some librarians address social justice issues as helping certain populations who are disadvantaged, while others try to ameliorate issues of social exclusion (R. G. Johnson, 2009; Pateman & Vincent, 2010). Librarians can also view social justice as an educational challenge, making patrons aware of biases, politics, and hegemonic influences and by directly supporting and facilitating other political or professional movements using the data and skills of librarianship, such as Radical Reference and the library of Occupy Wall Street (OWS) (Gregory & Higgins, 2013; Morrone, 2014). Concerns have been raised, though, about how well librarians have been prepared by their professional educations to serve in these social justice roles (Pateman & Vincent, 2010; Wilson & Birdi, 2008).

Toni Samek (2005, 2007) has identified a number of key links between librarianship and the UDHR:

- Respect for dignity of human beings (Article 1)
- Confidentiality (Articles 1, 2, 3, 6)

- Equality of opportunity (Articles 2, 7)
- Privacy (Articles 3, 12)
- Protection from torture and inhumane treatment (Article 5)
- Property (Article 17)
- Freedom of thought (Article 18)
- Freedom of expression (Article 19)
- Freedom to assemble and associate (Article 20)
- Development and dignity (Article 22)
- Education (Article 26)
- Cultural life of community (Article 27)
- Intellectual property (Article 27)

While these are all clear connections, similar connections also exist in the articles not noted in this list. In the age of the Internet, wirelessness, and social media, every aspect of the UDHR either relies on information or is enhanced by information.

Librarianship, however, also faces limitations in its ability to fulfill their human rights and social justice goals that extend far beyond a lack of recognition of their roles. "The human rights regime of a country is, at its foundation, political, because it is about the definite allocation of rights, resources, and responsibilities within a community" (Lazer, 2012, p. 244). For libraries, much of what they can achieve has been shaped by policy, political, and economic decisions in which they are typically not allowed to participate (Jaeger, Gorham, Bertot, & Sarin, 2014). For example, in the United States—as well as other nations such as Denmark—the role of social guarantor of Internet access and education is undermined by national policies that mandate filtering of the content that can be accessed through library computers (Jaeger & Yan, 2009; Jorgensen, 2006b).

Librarians also face challenges in articulating a larger philosophy toward rights and justice. In terms of information, rights and justice can be conceived in various ways, such as:

- distribution to meet all basic needs;
- equal distribution of all available resources;
- individuals receiving the benefits that they have personally earned;
- providing the greatest benefits to the least advantaged individuals; or
- favoring the benefits to society over the benefits to the individual (Rioux, 2010).

Each of these philosophies would create a different set of approaches for libraries to implement in trying to promote human rights and social justice.

Perhaps the greatest challenge for libraries as institutions of human rights and social justice is that they are trying to succeed in ways that the international infrastructure has not. "Human rights have succeeded in combating totalitarianism and preventing atrocities but have proved less able to promote a good life for people suffering less spectacular wrongs" (Moyn, 2012, n.p.). For libraries, the promotion of rights and justice occurs primarily at the individual and local community levels—supporting education, teaching digital literacy, building career skills, helping with the creation of a small business, and protecting the rights of community members, among many other smaller-scale but extremely important activities.

The focus on the relationships between human rights and social and political actors and the conditions to best promote the success of human rights in social and political contexts have been "missing from the study of human rights" (Nash, 2009, p. 1). Yet, according to the social connection model of community responsibility, all agents in a community—whether individual or institutional—have a responsibility to develop structural processes that promote rights and justice in the community (Young, 2006). Libraries have embraced this responsibility, even if it has not been widely studied, and are generally committed and innovative in these roles as institutions of human rights and social justice. The next chapter provides an extended view of the library as an institution that is inherently dedicated to rights and justice, in spite of the challenges presented by the surrounding political and social climate.

Chapter Four

Libraries as Institutions Promoting Human Rights and Social Justice

The library community is no stranger to doubts about the need for libraries in the age of Google (Kniffel, 2010). When the types of media containing information were limited in their availability and capacity, it was easy to see the necessity of libraries. After all, it would be extraordinarily expensive for anyone to own every book on every subject. The distribution of information materials on a community level enabled individuals to have greater access to information than possible on his or her own. Since the advent of the Internet, however, it has been much easier for critics to deride the need for libraries as the vast majority of the public's information needs can now seemingly be met so long as one has a broadband connection and an Internet device (Davlantes, 2010; Siegler, 2013). As one blogger opined, "The Internet has replaced the importance of libraries as a repository for knowledge. And digital distribution has replaced the role of a library as a central hub for obtaining the containers of such knowledge: books. And digital bits have replaced the need to cut down trees to make paper and waste ink to create those books" (Siegler, 2013, n.p.). Ignoring for a moment issues of access, this point of view might be reasonable if one accepted the argument that libraries are defined by their distribution of goods.

This definition ignores, however, the role of the library as: (1) a source of education and services, (2) an equalizing force in society, and (3) a symbol of equity and justice, as will be discussed more extensively in chapter 7. From the library community's adoption of service roles for immigrants in the early twentieth century to the digital literacy and inclusion, government services, job training, and access to food offered at the beginning of the next, libraries have demonstrated their role as institutions of education, public discourse, and equality (McCook, 2002; Thompson et al., 2014). The unique actions in

communities that define the library can be summarized as: informing, enabling, equalizing, and leading (Bertot, 2014). Such actions occur in many
different contexts: education, inclusion, employment, social services, public
spaces, digital literacy, and community development, as well as other community needs (Jaeger, Taylor, Gorham, Kettnich, Sarin, & Peterson, 2014).

This chapter discusses the differences between distributing goods that
contain information and offering the tools needed to access and use the
information itself. The meaning of a library has matured over time into being
inherently a "place of ideas" (Leckie & Buschman, 2007, p. 16). By expanding on the conception that libraries are institutions of human rights and social
justice regardless of the media formats they provide, this chapter embraces
the concept of libraries "becoming what they already are" by exploring libraries' historical and current practices. Various types of libraries—public,
school, academic, and special—illustrate the vast impact that libraries have
on all types of communities. A key thread woven into this discussion is the
relationship between libraries and their communities and the ways that libraries serve as the main (and often only) community information access point.
By describing examples of innovative library programs and services, this
chapter seeks to demonstrate the fact that libraries are the best institutions to
promote and advance equality of access to, education about, and services
related to information. In short, libraries are—and have always been—about
services rather than stuff. The stuff—from print materials to computer workstations and Wi-Fi—is clearly important and necessary for what libraries can
achieve in their communities, but the services are what makes libraries utterly unique and irreplaceable in their communities. There are, it seems, nearly
as many ways that libraries help their communities through community-
specific services as there are libraries (Brimhall-Vargas, 2015; Jaeger,
Cooke, Feltis, Hamiel, Jardine, & Shilton, 2015).

INSTITUTIONS OF EDUCATION

Historically, education has been a central role of all types of libraries (Stone,
1953). As early as 1876, in an issue of *American Library Journal*, Melville
Dewey wrote, "The time *was* when a library was very like a museum, and a
librarian was a mouser in musty books, and visitors looked with curious eyes
at ancient tomes and manuscripts. The time *is* when a library is a school, and
the librarian is in the highest sense a teacher" (Dewey, 1876, p. 6, italics in
original). Education is also one of librarianship's core values; as stated in the
ALA's policy manual, the association "promotes the creation, maintenance,
and enhancement of a learning society . . . [and] support[s] comprehensive
efforts to ensure that school, public, academic, and special libraries in every
community cooperate to provide lifelong learning services to all" (ALA,

2014b, n.p.). The range of learning needs across the lifespan that are represented in the examples below showcase the vital role that libraries play in their communities, particularly as the users who most need these services are those who are frequently already disadvantaged by society.

Libraries and Adult Education

In the 1920s, William S. Learned presented his influential report to the Carnegie Corporation that "set forth a concept of the public library as a 'community intelligence center,'" which prompted the ALA to appoint a Commission on the Library and Adult Education in 1924 (Stone, 1953, pp. 439–440). Today, libraries offer both formal and informal education-oriented programming in such diverse areas as basic literacy, language learning, job seeking, and computer training.

The 2003 National Assessment of Adult Literacy found that 14 percent of, or thirty million, adult Americans demonstrated a below basic prose literacy—defined as no more than the most simple and concrete literacy skills, which is considered less than the basic level of being able to perform simple and everyday literacy activities—highlighting the clear need for institutions of adult learning (National Center for Education Statistics, 2003). Training in basic literacy skills is offered in more than a third of public libraries (33.2 percent), while over a fourth (27.1 percent) offer GED or equivalency programs (Bertot, Jaeger, et al., 2014). Programs like the Californian Oakland Public Library's Second Start, which "offers a confidential setting in which adults with low skill levels are able to get a 'second start' at learning, for free" help fill this gap (Oakland Public Library, 2014). In addition to English language instruction, approximately 10 percent of all public libraries offer foreign language instruction (Bertot, Jaeger, et al., 2014).

By and large, however, the focus of adult education–oriented programming in public libraries tends to center around technology training. Although the popular conceptualization of the digital age is that everyone is online, around 15 percent of Americans do not use the Internet at all (Zickuhr, 2013b). Of this 15 percent, around one-third avoid being online because "it is difficult or frustrating to go online, they are physically unable, or they are worried about other issues such as spam, spyware, and hackers" (Zickuhr, 2013b, p. 2). These numbers are significant because they represent a sizable number of Americans who are left out of the social and economic benefits of the Internet. The library plays a significant role in providing training and access to those who want to be online but lack the technology and/or digital literacy to successfully participate. In fact, the expectation for this service is so great that digitalliteracy.gov includes a large sidebar on the "Learn the Basics" page that advertises, "Need in-person help? Find your local library!" and more than a third (36 percent) of those who have ever visited a library have received either computer- or Internet-related help from a librarian (Zickuhr, Rainie, & Purcell, 2013).

The public library community has responded to this need in creative and expansive ways. In a 2013–2014 survey, nearly every library (98 percent) reported offering some type of technology training (Bertot, Jaeger, et al., 2014). More than three-fourths of libraries indicated that they provide informal point-of-use training for general computer skills (79.9 percent), general software use (82.9 percent), and Internet use (81.6 percent) (Bertot, Jaeger, et al., 2014). In addition, specific populations benefit from targeted programs. For example, when less than half of seniors have a high-speed broadband connection at home and 41 percent are not online (Smith, 2014), it becomes critical to target the particular needs of these users. For older adults, these needs include accommodations for disabilities or socialization into the world of the Internet and demonstrations of how it might be relevant to their lives. Libraries have developed several program models to address these issues. For example:

- The Pasco County Library System in Florida trains teen technology tutors to help older adults with basic computer skills (Zickuhr, 2013a).
- The Old Bridge Public Library in New Jersey has created a specific space in the library devoted to the senior population, which includes a computer training center, among other resources ("Senior Spaces," n.d.).
- The Alameda County Library in Fremont, California, has both computer classes and intergenerational technology instruction as part of its older adult services (which also includes Wii bowling for seniors) (ALA, 2010a).

Those with physical disabilities also have unique needs, particularly accessing accessible devices and software. This is a population that not only has the lowest levels of Internet usage in the United States but also is less than half as likely as the rest of the population to use a computer at home or to live in a household with Internet access (Dobransky & Hargittai, 2006; Jaeger, 2012). Libraries attempt to help these users through programs such as the "One-on-One Basic Computer Training for Visually Impaired (& Sighted) Individuals" offered by the George W. Covington Memorial Library in Mississippi (Zickuhr, 2013a) and the robust Adaptive Services program at the Washington, DC, Public Library, through which patrons can access adaptive technologies, receive training in these technologies, participate in groups and meet-ups, and use an "Internet Classroom," designed to help patrons learn adaptive technologies on their own (District of Columbia Public Library, n.d.). While these services cannot address all of the numerous accessibility problems encountered by persons with disabilities (Fox, 2004; Fox & Madden, 2005; Jaeger & Bowman, 2005; University of California, Los Angeles, 2003), for many persons with disabilities these programs and tools are the key to an online world that the general population takes for granted.

In general, classes that utilize technology beyond basic computer skills are some of the more popular education services offered by the public library, including maker spaces, or "places to create, build, and craft" ("Manufacturing Makerspaces," 2013, n.p.). These spaces are available in nearly a fourth of city and suburban libraries and around a tenth of those in town and rural locations (Bertot, Jaeger, et al., 2014). Often the equipment in these spaces, such as 3-D printers, is very expensive, which recalls the question of whether there is a need to share resources in the digital age. Indeed, "the cost factor is what makes a makerspace so appealing to library visitors—what one person cannot afford to purchase for occasional use, the library can buy and share with the community" ("Manufacturing Makerspaces," 2013, n.p.). In addition, many libraries offer formal training for skills such as digital photography and website development (Bertot, Jaeger, et al., 2014). The DC Public Library has even hosted "Accessibility Hackathons" that "bring together young adults with disabilities, and companies that develop accessibility solutions, to provide mentorship and create new adaptive technology solutions" (District of Columbia Public Library, 2013, n.p.).

Libraries and the Education of Children

Libraries also offer ample services for younger patrons. In fact, almost three-fourths of parents (70 percent) said their child visited a public library in the last year, more than half to do schoolwork (with higher incidence among older children, aged twelve to seventeen, at 77 percent) and nearly half to attend a library event (C. Miller, Zickuhr, Rainie, & Purcell, 2013). A 2009 study found that 61 percent of young people (fourteen- to twenty-four-year-olds) in households living below the federal poverty line used public library computers and the Internet (Becker et al., 2010, p. 2). Outside of the public library, studies on the impact of school libraries continually show their influence on student achievement, despite their cuts in funding over the past decade (New York Comprehensive Center, 2011).

It is difficult to argue against the connection between libraries and reading. According to a Pew survey, 84 percent of parents credit public libraries with helping their children to love reading (Miller, Zickuhr, Rainie, & Purcell, 2013) and almost all public libraries (98.4 percent) offer summer reading programs (Bertot, Jaeger, et al., 2014). In addition, ALA initiatives, such as "Every Child Ready to Read" and "Born to Read," often help families to foster literacy in their preschool-aged children. Library services for children, however, go beyond connecting readers to books. Libraries offer literacy education to young learners with special learning needs, such as children with autism and English language learners. Since 2013, Seattle Public Library has been offering "Sensory Story Times," which are designed for children under ten who are on the autism spectrum or who have sensory issues and involve exercise and music therapy, as well as toys to squeeze to aid in their concentration (Barack, 2014). School librarians similarly structure their services to better accommodate their students with special needs, including adapting library checkout policies, building a collection with multiple formats of materials, and seeking out additional professional training to better understand their students' needs (Subramaniam, Oxley, & Kodama, 2013).

Some national initiatives are embraced by both public and school libraries, such as "El día de los niños/El día de los libros (Children's Day/Book Day)," which promotes events that (among other goals) "nurture cognitive and literacy development in ways that honor and embrace a child's home language and culture [and] introduce families to community resources that provide opportunities for learning through multiple literacies" (ALA, 2013b). Other cultural programs developed by the public library community include "Dai Dai Xiang Chuan (Bridging Generations, a Bag at a Time)," a program held at public libraries in Cleveland, San Francisco, and Indiana, which was "designed to improve intergenerational literacy, cultural awareness, and life skills for immigrant families and families with adopted children from China and Chinese speaking countries," as well as "Reading Is Grand," a Chicago Public Library project that focused on the relationship between African American grandparents and their grandchildren (ALA, n.d.).

INSTITUTIONS OF PUBLIC DISCOURSE AND CIVIC INCLUSION

As community institutions, libraries engage citizens to interact with the important political, civic, and legal issues that may impact them. Part of their role in this area is to offer spaces and services for dialogue, and part is to facilitate efforts by members of the public to deal with these issues in their day-to-day lives.

Libraries as Places of Discourse

Civic engagement has a tremendous impact on communities, whether it is localized decisions on how the school system is run or broader issues of funding for public services. The library is a particularly well-suited incubator for discussions of both local and national issues. The Hartford Public Library in Connecticut found this to be such a robust area of interest that they created the Center for Civic Engagement, "established to support community change, foster development of a community vision, contribute to a stronger community and establish a civic engagement model . . . [that] builds on the library's long-standing commitment to civic engagement and connects diverse programs into a coordinated community-building strategy" (Hartford Public Library, 2013, p. 11). As part of the center, the library has developed an informational website on relevant local issues; a series of public programs on issues such as urban planning and education; a coalition to increase voter engagement; a series of diverse community dialogues on civic issues; and a volunteer and partnership program to carry out ideas that citizens bring to these dialogues and programs (ULC, 2012). Elsewhere, libraries in a midwestern state were part of a recent study in which they led forums in the library on a locally relevant but complex issue (high-speed Internet access). Through a survey administered after these forums, participants reported increased conversation about the topic with friends and family, as well as ISPs and community leaders, demonstrating how discourse that takes place in the library can have impacts that extend beyond the walls of the institution (Schenck-Hamlin, Han, & Schenck-Hamlin, 2014).

Of course, not every attempt by libraries to engage in civic discourse is characterized by such civility. During the late summer and fall of 2011, volunteer librarians—about half of which were professional librarians or archivists—set up the People's Library of Occupy Wall Street. They fought rain, media scrutiny, police moratoriums, and, eventually, destruction at the hands of police officers and city sanitation workers. Regardless of one's opinion of the overall movement, the library of OWS was an attempt to demonstrate "that a library cannot simply be a physical space; it must resonate with a societal and mental place" (J. Taylor & Loeb, 2014, p. 280). Those involved with it viewed the library as fundamental to the OWS protest, not only because of the materials in its collections but also because of how it functioned as "a space where someone can learn about political activism and protest" while also "enabl[ing] protestors to relax, talk to each other, and gain information about non-protest related issues" (Lingel, 2012, n.p.). While this particular effort did not have the desired outcome, the support for this library evidenced through donations, as well as the value ascribed to it within the OWS community, demonstrates the role of the library as an institution in building community and promoting civic responsibility—even if the institution is a building held up by cardboard.

Libraries Connecting Patrons to Government

Although e-government aims to connect citizens to government resources, time has shown that there is a strong need for intermediaries to assist with the technology and civic literacy knowledge needed to successfully navigate these resources (N. G. Taylor, Gorham, Jaeger, & Bertot, 2014; N. G. Taylor, Jaeger, McDermott, Kodama, & Bertot, 2012; N. G. Taylor, Jaeger, Gorham, Bertot, Lincoln, & Larson, 2014). The example mentioned above of the government's directive for users of the digitalliteracy.gov website to go to libraries for additional help is not a new phenomenon. Indeed, on their general websites, many government agencies instruct users to visit the local library if they need assistance related to the site (Jaeger & Bertot, 2011). Public libraries fill this gap; in 2011–2012, nearly all (more than 96 percent) of public libraries helped their patrons access e-government or apply for e-government services (Bertot, Gorham, Jaeger, & Taylor, 2012; Bertot, McDermott, Lincoln, Real, & Peterson, 2012). Many public libraries have expanded beyond point-of-need services and have implemented programs to address the range of skills needed to successfully engage in e-government activities. Two notable examples are:

- Alachua County, Florida: The public library shares space with a range of local government agencies, so that patrons using the library to fill out documents for public services have access to the agencies providing these services nearby (Blumenstein, 2009; N. G. Taylor, Jaeger, Gorham, Bertot, Lincoln, & Larson, 2014).
- Queens, New York: Shortly after the Department of State mandated that the diversity visa application process be completed online, Queens Library (working with the Mayor's Office of Immigrant Affairs) set up designated times at different branches during which immigrants were able to receive assistance with scanning photographs to be submitted with their applications (Yaniv, 2005).

Library Programs and Services for Self-Represented Litigants

The concept of equal access to justice—defined as "the ability to avail oneself of the various institutions, governmental and non-governmental, judicial and non-judicial, in which a claimant might pursue justice" (Galanter, 2009, p. 115)—is generally touted as one of the foundations of the American legal system. The maze of laws, processes, and rules that govern this system, however, can make it difficult for individuals to avail themselves of these institutions.

In recent years, there has been a steady increase in the number of individuals representing themselves in court—commonly referred to as pro se or self-represented litigants—particularly in certain areas of law, such as family law and landlord/tenant disputes (Landsman, 2009; Staudt & Hannaford, 2002). This increase is often attributed to both the supply and demand of civil legal services. Many self-represented litigants lack the financial resources to hire an attorney yet do not qualify for free services from legal services organizations (Hannaford-Agor & Mott, 2003; Sims, 2004; Swank, 2004; Zorza, 2009). At the same time, many of these legal services organizations do not have sufficient resources to provide assistance to every eligible individual (Legal Services Corporation [LSC], 2012). Thus, the civil legal services delivery system in the United States is failing for many, as evidenced by reports that 80 percent of the civil legal needs of the poor go unmet (Engler, 2011; Houseman, 2001; Landsman, 2009; Spieler, 2013).

It is more than just a matter of economics, however. It has been observed that the growing perception that lawyers are not always necessary to pursue a legal action can be traced to two related notions, namely, that "the 'Home Depot' do-it-yourself method applies to a lot more than house repairs and that in the Internet era, the 'noble amateur' can do just about anything as well as the expert" (Landsman, 2009, p. 445). The increasing amount of legal information to which laypeople now have access, due to the Internet and related ICTs (Berenson, 2001), encourages them to navigate the legal system without legal counsel (Hale-Janeke & Blackburn, 2008; Snukals & Sturtevant, 2007).

Courts have taken the lead in developing self-help programs to provide assistance to this group of litigants (Schwarz, 2004; Shepard, 2010; Van Wormer, 2007; Zorza, 2012). Assisting courts in these efforts are libraries and legal aid organizations. Well established as community access points, these organizations are instrumental in connecting self-represented litigants with the legal information they need by removing barriers created by geography, language, and technology (Acosta & Cherry, 2007; National Center for State Courts [NCSC], 2006; Self-Represented Litigation Network [SRLN], 2008; Zorza, 2009, 2010). Both public libraries and law libraries that are open to the public are natural partners in the provision of self-help and legal information services (NCSC, 2012; Warren, 2004; Zorza, 2010). Public libraries are more likely to be the initial point of contact, but staff may lack the necessary skills and experience to facilitate self-represented litigants' access to legal information (Fritschel, 2007) and may be unsure of the parameters of acceptable assistance to self-represented litigants (Zorza, 2010).

Law library staff members' familiarity with operating in a legal environment is highly advantageous—they are well versed in the law as well as the tools and resources that can help self-represented litigants understand the law; they understand the process of legal research; they can help users navigate the world of online legal information; they routinely make community service referrals; and they can navigate legal information websites (Houseman, 2001; SRLN, 2008; Warren, 2004). Although law librarians generally have a clear understanding of the distinction between legal advice and legal information (Pettinato, 2008), they may find themselves faced with patrons who want them to function as de facto attorneys (Hale-Janeke & Blackburn, 2008).

Through the development of partnerships with legal aid and other community-based organizations and courts to provide assistance to self-represented litigants, public libraries and law libraries are becoming an increasingly important part of the access to justice movement in the United States. Examples of collaboration include the following:

- The Travis County Law Library in Texas worked with the judges and the clerk of the court to develop a set of locally approved court forms (Fritschel, 2007). These forms are made available on TexasLawHelp.org, a statewide legal information website maintained by the Texas Legal Services Center and supported by the Texas Access to Justice Foundation and legal aid organizations throughout the state.
- Many of the technology-based legal self-help centers established by Illinois Legal Aid Online, a nonprofit organization that emerged out of a collaboration among Chicago-Kent College of Law, the Chicago Bar Foundation, and the Lawyers Trust Fund, are located in public libraries (Zorza, 2010).
- Central Minnesota Legal Services received a grant from the LSC, the largest funder of civil legal services in this country, to develop library–legal aid collaborations, including a statewide webinar series to train librarians on online legal resources.

In addition, librarians from public law libraries serve on statewide access to justice commissions in a number of states, including California, Illinois, Kentucky, Maryland, Massachusetts, Montana, New Mexico, Texas, and Washington. Librarians' growing involvement in the ongoing dialogue about transforming the rhetoric of "equal access to justice" into meaningful action demonstrates a willingness to engage in the broader social justice issues related to access to legal information.

INSTITUTIONS OF EQUALITY

Embedded in all of the above examples is the idea that libraries are open to all. Indeed, this is a distinguishing aspect of libraries, delineated through the Library Bill of Rights, which includes such language as "A person's right to use a library should not be denied or abridged because of origin, age, background, or views" and "Libraries that make exhibit spaces and meeting rooms available to the public they serve should make such facilities available on an equitable basis, regardless of the beliefs or affiliations of individuals or groups requesting their use" (ALA, 1996, n.p.). Public, academic, school, and special libraries are all expected to be inclusive of the communities they serve.

While the education and civic roles certainly embody this philosophy, represented by the multitude of populations served by the programs mentioned above, it is important to emphasize the unique role of libraries in providing equal access to and ability to use information. The existence of spaces open to every person (in a public library) or every student (in a school) or every community member (academic or special library) is not particularly common. While in the recent past there were multiple environments open to the public (e.g., town squares), these spaces are disappearing. For nearly one hundred years, libraries have been places of refuge for people from all walks of life, but this role is becoming even more important as similar spaces cease to exist. In this way, the physical institution fulfills an important and necessary role for human rights and social justice.

Viewing the library as a safe space is not a new concept. Equal access to libraries has also been fought for against some of society's largest prejudices. For example, many public libraries aim to reduce the barriers to access of undocumented immigrants by emphasizing what the library does need (e.g., an address, some form of ID) and structuring services accordingly. REFORMA, the National Association to Promote Library & Information Services to Latinos and the Spanish Speaking, published a tool kit to help librarians respond to anti-immigrant attitudes. In the tool kit, the association offers examples from practices adopted in Los Angeles, Minnesota, and Queens Public Libraries. Suggestions include relaxing the requirements for identification by allowing the use of Matricula Consular IDs (an identification card issued by the Mexican government through its consulates) or school IDs for younger children and implementing a policy that does not require users to explain their legal status when registering for a library card (REFORMA, 2006). The work of several round tables in the ALA, including the Social Responsibilities Round Table, the Ethnic & Multicultural Information Exchange Round Table, and the Gay, Lesbian, Bisexual, Transgender Round Table, among others, call attention to populations that might otherwise be underserved. Today, libraries offer specialized services for some of the nation's most vulnerable and isolated populations, including the homeless, the impoverished, and the incarcerated.

Libraries and the Homeless

A report by the Department of Housing and Urban Development estimates that, on a single night in January 2013, 610,042 people were homeless in the United States (Henry, Cortes, & Morris, 2013). A recent Reuters article pronounced U.S. libraries as the "front line in [the] fight against homelessness," offering many examples of outreach to and accommodations for the homeless, including a summer reading club at the Queens Library in New York City; haircuts, meals, and blood pressure screenings in Greensboro, North Carolina; a café staffed by the homeless in Philadelphia; and a parking lot for shopping carts and miscellaneous property in Madison, Wisconsin (Simpson, 2014). Some libraries provide services at homeless shelters, while others offer targeted events designed through partnerships with others in the community who provide services that the homeless might need, such as access to mental health providers, social workers, and job training (Collins,

Howard, & Miraflor, 2009; Mars, 2013). The ALA (2012b) highlights other innovative services such as:

- *Public Library Street Card—Resources for Help, Baltimore County, Maryland*: Through a partnership with a local nonprofit organization, this card lists information on a variety of resources relevant to the homeless population, including job, food, monetary, and emergency information.
- *Community Technology Center, Denver, Colorado*: The Community Technology Center at Denver Public Library sends staff to area shelters to provide job skills training, including interviewing and technology instruction, to homeless and low-income women. The service also provides bus tokens to participants so that, following the class, they can tour the main library and get library cards.
- *Homelessness—A Panel Discussion, San Jose, California*: At the San Jose Public Library, staff held a panel discussion to facilitate a dialogue about the needs of those experiencing homelessness, with the goal of improving services to this population. Following this event, staff created a website with resources and information compiled by attendees.
- *Winter Book Club, Traverse City, Michigan*: Through a partnership with a local shelter, the Traverse Area District Library offers book club meetings at the shelter.

In other programs aimed at helping the homeless and better integrating them into their communities, libraries have hired social workers to work with homeless patrons in the libraries, partnered with other community groups to build library branches in affordable housing complexes, created special programs for use in homeless shelters, started book clubs for homeless patrons, and served regular meals in library branches, among much else (Galan, 2011; Gehner, 2010; Lilienthal, 2011; Muggleton, 2013).

Moreover, outside of libraries, homelessness is rarely dealt with as an important issue except in rare occasions that bring attention to it in unusual ways, such as the highly controversial "Homeless Hotspots" project (Koepfler, Mascaro, & Jaeger, 2014). In that project, homeless residents of Austin were paid to serve as Wi-Fi hotspots for visitors during the South by Southwest Festival, with reactions ranging from viewing the project as dehumanizing the participants to it being seen as a major act of self-empowerment for the participants. The controversy around the project brought the topic of homelessness to national attention for a brief time, though much of this media attention focused on the varied reactions to the project itself (Koepfler, Mascaro, & Jaeger, 2014). The reactions surrounding the Homeless Hotspots project demonstrated that confused and negative attitudes toward the homeless clearly persist, driving home the importance of the library efforts described above to be a community institution that is genuinely trying to provide support to this marginalized population.

Library Programs and Services for Prisoners

At the end of 2012, the prisoner population was 1.57 million and the total correctional system population in the United States—which includes individuals on parole and probation—was 6.94 million (Bureau of Justice Statistics, 2013). Although there has been a decline in the number of admissions, as well as the total correctional population in recent years, about one in thirty-five adults is currently supervised by the adult correctional system. For those within this system, access to information takes on a new level of importance. A detailed examination of the civil rights afforded to prisoners is beyond the scope of the book; however, the notion of prisoners' intellectual freedom clearly demonstrates the connections between access to information, social justice, and human rights. The ALA's statement on *Prisoners' Right to Read* aptly captures this connection: "Participation in a democratic society requires unfettered access to current social, political, economic, cultural, scientific, and religious information. Information and ideas available outside the prison are essential to prisoners for a successful transition to freedom. Learning to be free requires access to a wide range of knowledge, and suppression of ideas does not prepare the incarcerated of any age for life in a free society" (ALA, 2014b, n.p.). Both prison libraries and public libraries have been instrumental in ensuring that prisoners are not denied access to information.

As originally conceived, prison libraries had three main purposes: religious and secular education; rehabilitation; and entertainment (Abel, 2013). It was not until the twentieth century that the idea of a prison law library came into being, focused on

> keeping inmates busy and thus out of trouble, convincing inmates their sentences were just, instilling in prisoners a greater respect for the law, helping to legitimize the criminal justice system, undermining the jailhouse lawyer's monopoly on legal information, and limiting supposedly frivolous litigation by convincing inmates that they had no legal grounds for complaint. (Abel, 2013, p. 1179)

The role of early prison law libraries thus did not include providing access to courts—this role developed throughout the twentieth century and has been the subject of an ongoing debate within the legal community.

This debate has been fueled by several Supreme Court decisions, namely, *Bounds v. Smith*, 430 U.S. 817 (1977) and *Lewis v. Casey*, 518 U.S. 343 (1996). In *Bounds*, the court established that prisoners have a constitutional right to access to courts and that prison law libraries were a key avenue for providing this access. Following this decision, the American Association of

Law Librarians (AALL) led the movement to develop suggestions for prison law library materials aimed at furnishing "adequate legal information to allow prisoners to litigate their convictions, their conditions of confinement, prison grievance issues, civil rights claims, and basic civil issues including custody, divorce, visitation, and termination of parental rights issues" (Trammell, 1997). Prison law libraries thus became a primary mechanism through which states fulfilled their constitutional obligation to provide prisoners with access to courts (E. S. Smith, 2010). *Bounds*, however, was not embraced by everyone in the legal community—criticism of this holding generally centered around the belief that prisoners generally lack the reading, writing, and research skills to effectively use the legal materials available in prison libraries (Chanen, 1998; Turner, 1979). Moreover, as described by Werner (1970) and C. E. Smith (1987), deficiencies in terms of both resources and staffing in prison libraries have been well documented.

As the number of lawsuits filed by prisoners increased significantly in the years following *Bounds*, prison law libraries became a target for those who deemed the bulk of these lawsuits to be frivolous (C. E. Smith, 1987). Against this backdrop, in *Lewis v. Casey*, the Supreme Court held that *Bounds* and its progeny did not create "an abstract, free-standing right to a law library or legal assistance." In the wake of *Lewis*, the very survival of prison law libraries was called into question, as some states moved to close them and/or placed extreme limits on prisoners' access to legal materials (Trammell, 1997). Nearly twenty years later, however, prison libraries continue to serve as an avenue for providing prisoners with access to courts, often through collaborative efforts with state law libraries. One notable example of such collaboration is Law Library Services to Prisoners, a project of the Minnesota State Law Library, through which librarians meet with prisoners to discuss their research needs, provide advice on conducting research in prison libraries, and deliver requested materials from the state libraries (E. S. Smith, 2010).

It is worth noting that prisoners' rights related to information extend beyond access to legal information, as clearly asserted in the ALA's Statement on Prisoners' Rights. Collaborations between prison libraries and public libraries have become an increasingly important mechanism for protecting prisoners' right to information in a wide range of areas (McCook, 2004; Klick, 2011). By way of example, in recent years, there has been an increased focus on providing services that can help prisoners as they transition back into society. Public and prison libraries have both undertaken initiatives to ease this reentry process, developing programs focused on the development of literacy and job seeking skills. Examples include a financial literacy program implemented at the Colorado Territorial Correctional Facility, involving modules to be completed on the library computer, and training sessions offered at the San Diego County Library for recent parolees to help them develop their job search, computer, and interview skills (Lilienthal, 2013).

LIBRARIES AND COMMUNITY ENGAGEMENT

A recent study found that only 14 percent of Americans are completely disengaged from libraries (Zickuhr & Rainie, 2014). For the vast majority of Americans who have some level of interaction with libraries, there seems to be a positive impact for other forms of community engagement. People who frequently use public libraries, for example, are also more likely to attend plays and concerts, patronize bookstores, and visit museums, galleries, and historical sites (Zickuhr & Rainie, 2014). These connections evidence the depth to which libraries are not only ingrained in their communities, but serve as engines of community engagement and interaction in areas as diverse as community gardens (e.g., the Library Farm at Northern Onondaga Public Library in New York that promotes food literacy and provides "fresh organic produce for local food pantries" [Zickuhr, 2013a]) and community nursing services (e.g., the Library Nurse Program at the Pima County Public Library in Arizona, that, through a partnership with the County Health Department, offers "on-site intervention services . . . [wherein] five nurses rotate among library branches for a total of 40 hours per week" [ULC, 2013]).

As the examples offered throughout this chapter demonstrate, libraries of all types regularly engage in a dramatically broad range of programs, services, outreach, and other activities to educate and engage their communities. The technological changes since the advent of the World Wide Web considerably expand the ability of libraries to provide social richness and innovation in their contributions to their communities (Maness, 2006). These library contributions to rights and justice are both formal and informal. Through their formal programs, services, outreach, and other planned activities, libraries provide "equity of access to information and the world of knowledge" (Kent, 1996, p. 209). Through providing an open community space, libraries promote "collaborative work" and "social activity" (Pomerantz & Marchionini, 2007, p. 505). Through informal interactions with individual patrons, libraries are "a trusted ear and an unbiased source of information and support to anyone who walks in the door" (Zabriskie, 2013, n.p.).

While they represent only a selection of relevant library activities, these actions and community contexts are the best ways by which to demonstrate the impressive contributions of libraries to their patrons, communities, local governments, local economies, and so much else. They also show that human rights and social justice considerations of many, many different types are central to innumerable library activities that benefit multitudinous groups in their communities and the communities as a whole. As one example, the ULC (2010) has written extensively about libraries as anchors of equity in their communities and as central to local sustainability for the economy, environment, and citizens. Yet, despite this clear understanding of everything that they do, the ULC does not label libraries as institutions of human rights and social justice. Overall, while actions of libraries resoundingly demonstrate their roles in rights and justice, libraries are extremely reluctant to describe their actions in terms of rights and justice. The next chapter explores this tension between words and actions.

Chapter Five

The Unspoken Roles of Libraries as Institutions of Human Rights and Social Justice

The previous chapter's examples demonstrate the various ways that libraries already act as institutions of human rights and social justice, and the professional literature is filled with cases and services that are human rights and social justice activities, even if they are not named as such. A paper on LGBTQ book clubs and public libraries (Pruitt, 2010) offers an excellent example of a very thoughtful paper about rights and justice issues that does not label them as such. This paper examines the ways in which LGBTQ patrons and causes can be—and are—supported by public libraries in their communities, as well as the ways in which libraries could better support LGBTQ patrons, with the support of gay men's book clubs as a key lens for the examination (Pruitt, 2010). That paper explores issues of policy, politics, access, inclusion, and education, but does not discuss them as rights and justice issues or the library roles as being rights and justice activities. Such a quandary is endemic to LIS discourse, with innumerable papers discussing some aspect of rights and justice in libraries without using the language of rights and justice.

In contrast, the ALA frequently uses language related to these concepts in professional guides and statements regarding the ideals of librarianship (McCook & Phenix, 2006), yet the terms are not widely used among library professionals. Why then, are libraries not promoted—or promoting themselves—in these terms? The bigger picture—that the institution of the library is one of the last few elements of the public good left standing—is rarely discussed by librarians or the general public. Libraries also fulfill many rights that would otherwise be unfulfilled, including the right to information, but still public discourse surrounding libraries rarely mentions these rights. There are various reasons for this discrepancy, stemming from both the library community's perception of itself and the broader economic forces at play in this country.

Within the profession, there have always been librarians that entered the field not because of their desire to serve but rather out of their love of books. While this is a small—and likely shrinking—minority, these librarians have a voice within library scholarship and beyond. In the popular media, one newspaper quotes a former president of the ALA, Michael Gorman, as saying, "If you want to have game rooms and pingpong tables and God knows what—poker parties—fine, do it, but don't pretend it has anything to do with libraries. . . . The argument that all these young people would turn up to play video games and think, 'Oh by the way, I must borrow that book by Dostoyevsky'— it seems ludicrous to me" (Sarno, 2010, n.p.). Again, these conceptualizations focus on the role of the library as a repository for books, or "enriching" materials, while minimizing the value of the diverse services provided by libraries.

Other voices within librarianship call for more limited services to fewer populations. For example, some members of the library community oppose the provision of services to the homeless. They believe that the presence of the homeless distracts from the experience for other patrons, and there is ongoing disagreement within the public library community on how to handle such issues as hygiene and property (Cronin, 2002; Mars, 2013). Another example of a minority voice within librarianship is support for censorship of materials and filtering of Internet access. In the case of filters, though the ALA aggressively fought against the implementation of the filtering requirements of CIPA, a large number of librarians, library systems, and even some state libraries actively supported filtering of Internet access for library patrons (Jaeger, McClure, Bertot, & Langa, 2005; Jaeger & Yan, 2009). Censorship in collection development historically was a key role of the library by choosing the "best reading" for patrons (Wiegand, 1999). Although the profession is largely opposed to such measures today, the desire to avoid controversy still affects collection decisions. For example, a 2009 *School Library Journal* survey found that almost three-fourths (70 percent) of respondents had been influenced not to purchase a book by the possible reaction of parents. Less common, but still prevalent, were those influenced by possible reactions from their administration (29 percent), the community (28 percent), and students (25 percent) (D. L. Whelan, 2009).

The way in which the education of library and information professionals has evolved certainly plays a role here. In the middle of the twentieth century, the library profession created the MLS degree as the standard degree requirement of the profession to create a uniform measure of preparedness for entering the profession (Swigger, 2012). This degree quickly had to adapt to a field that was becoming increasingly influenced by the perspectives of information science in education, which were more focused on technologies and systems than professionals and patrons (e.g., Borko, 1968; Miles, 1967; R. S. Taylor, 1962). Educators preparing future librarians still are struggling to reconcile these tensions. For many who favor a greater focus on the professionals and the patrons, the growing influence of information science— and related areas such as human computer interaction (HCI)—threatens to end library education (e.g., Cox, 2011; Dilevko, 2009; Swigger, 2012).

Since the mid-1990s, one of the so-called crises in LIS education has stemmed from concern that curricular offerings and requirements were not sufficiently oriented to the needs of practitioners (Dillon & Norris, 2005). One of the responses to this perceived crisis has been to focus on defining the core components of an LIS educational program (Hall, 2009; Markey, 2004). Markey (2004), for example, concluded that typical course offerings can be grouped into five broad categories: organization; reference; foundations; management; and research methodology of information technology. None of these categories reflect the social services and education roles of librarianship today.

Moreover, this focus on the perceived lack of a core curriculum for the discipline may have created a deeper divide between the ideals of the profession and its practice. As asserted by H. L. M. Jacobs and Berg:

> The ALA Core Values seem to have lost their traction or relevance in the daily work librarians perform . . . [which] may relate to the primary focus of librarians' education being primarily upon the required skills, tools, and the technologies related to librarianship rather than the social aspects outlined in documents like the Alexandria Proclamation or the ALA Core Values. (2011, p. 391)

In particular, with the notable exceptions discussed in chapter 7, there is little emphasis within the curriculum of LIS programs on how these skills, tools, and technologies promote social justice and human rights.

This focus on the more practical aspects of librarianship had implications for the profession as a whole, as well as for LIS education. During the early to mid-twentieth century, the ALA was making grand statements to guide the library community through seminal documents such as the Library Bill of Rights, adopted in 1939, and the Freedom to Read Statement, adopted in 1953 (ALA, 1996, 2004b). In the 1960s, however, several of these ideals were found to be wanting in practice. Culminating with the organization of the Social Responsibilities Round Table in 1969, many of ALA's members argued against

> the principle of "neutrality" most often advocated by veteran librarians[,] an excuse not to address inequities in library practice caused by racism, sexism,

and homophobia, a rationale not to confront a government bent on conducting
a unjust war in southeast Asia, and a mechanism to give the Library Bill of
Rights a strict construction that rendered it ineffective in the fight to include
alternative perspectives in library collections. (Wiegand, 1999, p. 19)

In addition, many of the statements in favor of equal rights to information
were found to be ignored in practice (McCook & Phenix, 2006).

Following these events, the profession began to shift to local planning
models and measurement (McCook & Phenix, 2006). This shift occurred
partially because it was thought to be a way that the idealistic views of
librarianship could actually be implemented. As more attention was focused
on this form of planning and assessment, however, overarching philosophies
became buried in practicalities. In 1979, the profession rejected a Public
Library Mission Statement designed to push librarians to work for a totally
egalitarian society (McCook, 2004; McCook & Phenix, 2006). As this shift
was occurring, however, there were also larger forces at work in the country
that made outcome-oriented planning preferable to philosophical rationales
for change.

The economic climate in the country has played a tremendous role in how
the value of information is discussed, which in turn has affected how libraries
operate. This has only increased since the 1980s. Sheldon Wolin describes a
shift from political rhetoric and belief informed by intellectual and philosophical groundings (e.g., English common law and the Enlightenment) to a
political landscape that places enormous emphasis on the economy and capitalism (Wolin, 1981). Because this grounding is so influential to the rhetoric
that surrounds information policy decisions and, thus, libraries, the various
economic forces that impede the mission of the library field, as well as the
ways in which they affect the field's message, will now be examined. This
discussion will also shed light on why librarians struggle to conceptualize
themselves as institutions promoting human rights and social justice, in an
effort to explain the disconnect between actions and messages.

THE PUBLIC SPHERE IN THE FREE MARKET

Though the events discussed above are indeed prime precursors to the outcome-based assessment models of the twenty-first century, as early as the
1920s library scholars were arguing for outcome-based assessment. In 1920,
John Cotton Dana said all public institutions "should give returns for their
cost; and those returns should be in good degree positive, definite, visible,
measurable. . . . Common sense demands that a publically supported institution do something for its supporters and that some part at least of what it does
be capable of clear description and downright valuation" (Dana, 1999, as
cited in R. S. Martin, Blalock, Wells, & Wolf, 2006, p. 191). The United

States is a country simultaneously built on democratic ideals and capitalism, creating an inherent tension between promoting the public good and promoting a free market. As a result of these long-standing tensions, throughout the country's history, periods of increased public support have generally been pushed against by those in favor of increased market control and a smaller government. This phenomenon was exemplified in the 1920s with the removal of many Progressive Era reforms, as well as during the post–Great Society era of Ronald Reagan and the rise of the conservative movement. In the years since the Great Society, the United States has seen growing opposition to social services in political circles. As the public sphere shrinks due to this opposition, it becomes all the more important for the library to articulate its value in this increasingly hostile environment.

WHAT IS VALUE?

Value is a loaded term that can be defined in many ways. For example, the library community is known for the value it places on reading. Conceptualized in this way, value could be characterized as something "good" for the person to be reading, whether it is in terms of personal happiness or increased skills that will serve an economic or academic purpose. Both conceptualizations depend on certain ideologies. For example, for these value statements to be correct, one must believe people enjoy reading or that the reader desires the job or schooling that the reading will support. The library profession also has overarching values—those that are not economic but still major contributions to their communities in other ways—including stances on such issues as access, confidentiality and privacy, democracy, diversity, education, intellectual freedom, preservation, the public good, professionalism, service, and social responsibility (ALA, 2004a). These core values are represented in the committees and special interest groups of the ALA and seminal documents produced by the association, such as the aforementioned Library Bill of Rights, and again represent a distinct notion of how such stances will benefit those that librarians serve.

When library professionals, educators, and researchers talk about the value of public institutions such as libraries, there is a tendency to focus on their contributions to social welfare in a somewhat abstract manner. Mark Moore, in his seminal *Creating Public Value: Strategic Management in Government* (1995), makes the concept of "public value" more concrete. He describes how a librarian might best approach the goal of achieving value for his or her public:

> The public librarian begins thinking as society expects private executives to think. She focuses on the question of whether the bundle of assets and capabilities represented by the library can be used to create additional value for the

town. She does not assume that her resources are immutably fixed, or that her
mission is narrowly and inflexibly inscribed in stone, or that her organization
is capable of producing only what it is now producing. (p. 18)

This is, in fact, often how librarians have responded to changes over the last
century, innovating programs, introducing new technology, and adapting
their role to fit the times.

The real concern with this approach to public value is the emphasis on
modeling private sector firms. Underlying the theory of public value is the
idea that public institutions are similarly interested in "getting the most out of
the bundle of assets entrusted to them by figuring out the best use of the
assets, and finding ways to produce their products and services or achieve
their desired social results at the lowest possible cost" (Moore & Khagram,
2004, p. 5). While libraries do sometimes operate in terms of assets or goods
(e.g., checking out books, allowing patrons to use spaces), they also operate
in ideas. Information and education are difficult to quantify in the same way
a business might assess returns on widgets, and yet attempts to commodify
information persist.

As early as 1962, with the publication of *The Production and Distribution
of Knowledge in the United States*, Fritz Machlup identified the United
States' shift to a "knowledge economy." With this shift, information is
viewed as a product and/or a service, and the ability to measure its inputs and
outputs becomes an important issue. When thinking about information in the
context of human rights and social justice, however, relying entirely on an
approach to valuation focused on inputs and outputs misses the forest for the
trees. Like many aspects of information, the rights to access and understand
information and the rights derived from information cannot be ascribed a
price. When libraries are providing services in support of social justice and
human rights that no other institution offers, the evaluation demands an
entirely different set of foci on entirely different measurements (an issue that
is revisited in chapter 7).

Nonetheless, the commodification of information has important implications for library services, particularly in how the library community frames
its roles. This is evidenced by the fact that, over the past two decades,
libraries have been increasingly referring to patrons as customers (Auld,
2004; Budd, 1997) and constructing neoliberal explanations for their educative role, such as conceptualizing information literacy as a tool for job readi-
ness (Enright, 2013). As noted library scholar Jesse Shera (1949) wrote, "The
objectives of the library are directly dependent on the objectives of society
itself" (p. 248). While this statement obviously can be viewed through the
lens of libraries serving community needs, it also reminds us that libraries are
beholden to monetary and political support to ensure their continued existence.

As libraries are encouraged by funders and academics alike to define their value in economic terms, their evaluation efforts, particularly in academic libraries, are increasingly focused on financial value or the value of returns (Oakleaf, ACRL, & ALA, 2010). Technology has also contributed to this transformation, wherein services are defined by a top-down vision of the information economy. "To the extent that people's 'information economy' does not require use of these technologies within the culture in which they live, current 'information science' discourse renders them and their culture(s) invisible largely by ignoring both" (Wiegand, 1999, p. 25). Even if people do value technology, it may be different from the prevailing corporate notion of why that technology has value. As one observer noted:

> Libraries need technology, but we must recognize that the values driving "startup culture" and most technology companies are radically different from the values librarians have held and defended for decades. Librarians value preservation, privacy, and sharing. Startups and tech corporates value growth, extracting and profiting from personal data and, quite literally, selling out. (Rundle, 2014, n.p.)

One concern with the shift to outcome-based assessment is the perpetual political problem of the tyranny of the majority. When we ask libraries to serve their communities, it can be difficult to parse what that means in practice. As some believe, being "perceived as advocates for community solutions" means that

> we need to align ourselves with the agendas of our elected officials and re-source allocators. Whether it is the local councilman whose primary priority is economic development, the congressperson who is most interested in work-force development in his district, or the University provost who wants to provide demonstrable measure of teaching and learning achievement on her campus, libraries can offer indispensable assistance in achieving these goals. We should strive to find the appropriate place for the library at the tables where decisions about these issues are being made. (R. S. Martin, Blalock, Wells, & Wolf, 2006, p. 192)

However, even if libraries are able to carve out a place for themselves at decision-making tables, they are still likely to struggle with *what* to say. Should they advocate for decisions to serve the greatest number of citizens? Those who frequent the library most often? Those who hold the purse strings? Those to whom public library services matter the most?

This latter group, however, includes the poor, immigrants, the homeless, the unemployed, those with lower levels of education, older adults, persons with disabilities, and other groups whose needs rarely make it onto the agenda of the elected officials or resource allocators. Further, the ability of each of these groups to lobby on their own behalf is hampered by a lack of both disposable income and political skills (Baumgartner, Berry, Hojnacki, Leech, & Kimball, 2009). Birkland (2001) defines the public policy agenda as "a collection of problems, understandings of causes, symbols, solutions and other elements of public problems that come to the attention of members of the public and their governmental officials" (p. 106). Baumgartner et al. (2009), in suggesting that there is a systemic bias in the policy-making process in this country, focus on the importance of agenda setting. In their study of one hundred issues across a range of activities in the federal government, they found that individual corporations, trade associations, and professional groups—all of whom are generally relatively wealthy—tended to be the main issue identifiers. They also observed that there was "a relative paucity" of issues relating to economic issues affecting the poor and the working class in their sample (p. 255).

This raises the question of whether policy makers even strive to produce an egalitarian society. In 1849, education reformer Horace Mann wrote that

> nothing but universal education can counterwork this tendency to the domina-
> tion of capital and the servility of labor. If one class possesses all the wealth
> and the education, while the residue of society is ignorant and poor, it matters
> not by what name the relation between them may be called: the latter, in fact
> and in truth, will be the servile dependents and subjects of the former. (Mann,
> 1952, p. 59)

In a country supposedly so dedicated to the American dream, the gap between the rich and the poor continues to grow. In fact, in 2013, the wealth gap between the richest 1 percent of Americans and the 99 percent below was the largest in almost a century (Stewart, 2013). Recent policies to boost the economy after the Great Recession only seem to be adding to this discrepancy (Leubsdorf, 2014).

The allocation of limited resources is always a tenuous proposition, and libraries are thus put in the position of having to convince those who fund them of the value of their services to these groups that are all too often invisible to policy makers. The stakes are incredibly high as failure in this arena will inevitably lead to a library that does not promote equality. While the economy has changed from the industrial model to a knowledge-based one, it seems some divides remain the same, despite the development of public education. Notwithstanding their continued commitment to ensuring equal access to information, librarians' struggle to define their contributions in a manner that resonates with policy makers and funders has undoubtedly made it more difficult for them to demonstrate how social justice– and human rights–related activities fit into their professional lives. Not surprisingly, politicians who favor reducing library funding or closing library branches are typically unaware of the socioeconomic contributions of libraries (Svendsen, 2013). While there have been numerous public movements to provide library-related assistance outside of the institution itself, such as Radical Reference and the OWS library, these fledgling activist groups have often failed without the support of a stable organization. And, though the ALA has acknowledged these outside roles in various special interest groups, subcommittees, and conference presentations, this type of justice- and rights-oriented work is most often conducted entirely outside of the professional library setting.

The official library community's response—largely carried out by ALA—has fallen more along the lines of making declarations at national conferences, sending out mass e-mails for members to call their elected representatives or sign petitions, and participating one day a year in National Library Legislation Day. Some may argue that this is necessary, perhaps libraries should not embrace what may be seen as "radical" activities with taxpayer funds. But, if we do desire the library to continue its role as a truly civic institution, it is precisely these sorts of discussions that should be occurring within the library community. The forums on broadband discussed in chapter 4 were intentionally apolitical, but the ability to engage in and facilitate controversial information-related discussions only adds to the library's uniqueness as a cultural institution. The separation of such advocacy from other professional roles has led to an odd dichotomy in which librarians are clearly doing justice- and rights-related work embedded in programming, services, and outreach, but not generally discussing their professional activities in these terms. Tellingly, in surveys of local politicians about public libraries, a majority believe that libraries themselves hurt their own support by inadequate marketing, a lack of advocacy, differences in operational structure, and isolation from the rest of government (Wooden, 2006).

Some in the community of library professionals fail to address the issue entirely, either because they do not believe it is particularly central to their job or because they do not think about the issues at all. However, the community has generally conceptualized their professional roles as one of teachers of information literacy (in which social justice and human rights are embedded), supporters of social justice and human rights (offering services for other movements), and workers in a larger infrastructure of social support (forming partnerships with other organizations). Each of these roles is undeniably important, but librarians are much more than workers on the sidelines of these issues. Narrowly defining the librarian's role in rights-based issues is a dangerous path to follow, not only because it allows others to forget what libraries do, but also because it allows the field to slowly drift from its core values.

TEACHERS OF THE SKILLS FOR THE TWENTY-FIRST CENTURY

Some librarians view their contribution to social justice and human rights as their role in teaching various skills necessary to succeed in the twenty-first century. The American Association of School Librarians (AASL) and the Association of College and Research Libraries (ACRL) both provide guides for what students need to know in the digital age, emphasizing school and academic librarians' educative role. These standards, the Standards for the 21st-Century Learner for K–12 students and Information Literacy Competency Standards for Higher Education for college-aged students, represent the perceptions that the "knowledge" or "information" age requires a different set of skills to succeed and that librarians fill a role in teaching students these skills.

The Standards for the 21st-Century Learner emphasize such themes as "global awareness; financial, economic, business, and entrepreneurial literacy; civic literacy; [and] health literacy" (AASL, 2009, p. 9). Alongside such general skills as creativity, critical thinking, flexibility, and responsibility, among others, the standards also emphasize information, media, and ICT literacies. The ACRL standards, adopted in 2000, place even greater emphasis on information literacy, describing it as "increasingly important in the contemporary environment of rapid technological change and proliferating information resources" (ACRL, 2000, p. 2). Currently under revision, the next iteration of the guidelines looks to continue to place the role of the academic librarian as central to the growth of the scholar in a new age of information.

However, there are those that would argue against this current conception of information literacy (Enright, 2013; H. L. M. Jacobs & Berg, 2011). Instead of showing the personal abilities enabled by technology and information skills, these critics believe that the entire concept of information literacy is neoliberal in focus, because of the relation of the language of skills to the ideology of maximizing the worker's economic potential (Enright, 2013). More specifically, H. L. M. Jacobs and Berg assert that "the teaching of information literacy . . . is often divorced from pedagogical or social theories and is often taught as something inseparable from the ACRL standards" (2011, p. 391). Allowing standards to define the parameters of what librarians are teaching does carry with it the problem of a narrow conceptualization of the impact of this teaching.

Numerous examples in the last chapter show the clear need that disadvantaged populations have for the types of skills taught by libraries, lending support to the notion that this instruction does, in fact, contribute to a more knowledgeable workforce and more autonomous citizens. From basic computer skills, to reading instruction, to guides for evaluating resources, this education reaches individuals who have had limited educational opportunities while also empowering people in a way that is often not possible within the confines of a classroom, particularly with the amount of required curriculum in today's education environment. It is possible, however, that by qualifying these standards as linked to formal institutions of education and situated within a neoliberal economic framework, librarians themselves fail to see a clear link between the skills, social justice, and human rights.

SUPPORTERS OF THE MOVEMENT

Other librarians go beyond their role as teachers and instead conceive of themselves as supporters of movements related to social justice and human rights. The aforementioned Radical Reference group, begun in 2006, is a prime example of this type of role. According to their website, the group, made up of volunteer library workers, has "answered questions that have ranged in scope from mail tampering in prison to the history of radical education to the future of librarianship" (Radical Reference, 2013). Their mission is to support "activist communities, progressive organizations, and independent journalists by providing professional research support, education and access to information" (Radical Reference, 2013). While the group suspended reference services in 2013 due to time constraints, members continue to support local activists and maintain their website.

Of course support does not have to be this explicit. As this book was being written, the news was brimming with reports from Ferguson, Missouri, where a young, unarmed black male was shot to death by a white policeman. In an example of continued racial injustice and unrest in this country, the community protested both the shooting itself and the police response to the shooting. Curfews were enacted in the town and police actively sought to shut down protests. During this activity, the local library advertised through social media that it offered a quiet place to review e-mails and get refreshments. Later, teachers would use the library space to offer activities for the town's youth, out of school after the start of the school year was delayed for a week. In its messaging, the library emphasized that it was there for the people of Ferguson, demonstrated by a sign outside its building: "Stay strong Ferguson. We are family" (Curry & Grimes, 2014).

These examples both clearly show how librarians cast themselves in supporting roles for the promotion of human rights and social justice. The question is, however, why are such activities not considered activism in and of themselves?

LIBRARIANS AS PARTNERS

Some librarians view their roles as partners, operating within networks of institutions providing services in support of rights and justice. These partnerships are designed to meet specific community needs more effectively than the institutions can on their own. Partnerships are indeed the key to moving forward in establishing libraries' roles in their communities, but we should not make the mistake of downgrading libraries' contributions to these partnerships.

These partnership programs vary across the country, meeting unique local community needs. Often, the resulting partnerships are quite innovative. In Baltimore, Maryland, the public libraries worked with the City Health Department to ensure the availability of fresh groceries to those living in food deserts by providing opportunities for patrons to order their groceries through library computers and pick up the food from the library the next day. In Alachua County, Florida, Alachua County Library District, working with the local office of the state's Department of Children and Families, the Partnership for Strong Families, and Casey Family Programs, opened a 4,500-square-foot space that, in addition to the library, houses approximately forty nonprofit organizations and local government agencies that provide social services focused on child welfare, greatly facilitating an individual's ability to work with all of the interrelated agencies to get needed support as quickly as possible. These are but two notable examples of a great many across the nation.

Other examples of this practice were discussed in chapter 4, including the Center for Civic Engagement (Hartford Public Library, Connecticut); the Library Nurse Program (Pima County Public Library, Arizona); and the Winter Book Club (Traverse Area District Library, Michigan). In engaging in services of this nature, librarians begin to see how the work they do intersects with social justice and human rights. It is necessary, however, for them to go a step further and begin to conceive of the library itself as an institution of social justice and human rights. Libraries act not only as support mechanisms within these partnerships, but as essential members of teams that fulfill roles no other institution is capable of doing. In the case of the American Place in Hartford, Connecticut, the role that the library plays in serving as both a safe space for immigrants and a knowledge center for this community is unique. Not only does the American Place provide information and resources for new immigrants, but the entire application process for residency and citizenship flows through the library. The library evens hosts citizenship swearing-in ceremonies.

LIBRARIES IN SOCIETY

Libraries do not operate within a vacuum—what they do is influenced by the individuals who staff them as well as broader economic and political forces. And, as society changes in response to these external forces, public institutions should adapt accordingly. Libraries have struggled, however, as these forces are increasingly asking them to define their value in terms of costs and benefits. Because libraries cannot quantify their commitment to the ideals espoused by the ALA or the profession's other fundamental philosophical beliefs, the prevailing economic forces have put them in an untenable position. As they struggle to come up with some way to demonstrate their value in quantifiable terms, libraries are given fewer and fewer opportunities to think of their work as promoting human rights and social justice, despite the fact that an increasing number of the roles they fulfill fall squarely into this realm.

The result of the disconnect between what the field says it is, what society thinks it is, and what libraries actually do is a profession that is continually fighting for funding and respect, while simultaneously fulfilling a diverse array of community needs. This is largely a perception problem, particularly among those in the policy environment, and it falls on librarians to try to reconcile these gaps. As J. Taylor and Loeb (2014) write:

> When people thinking about libraries think first of books, they are taking a logical step; however, it falls to librarians to remind patrons that the library represents much more. Access to a library is important, not simply because it provides access to information, but because access to a library represents access to an information commons as well as a belief that people have a right to such access. (p. 280)

Later chapters return to the responsibility of librarians to embrace their roles in the human rights and social justice arenas, but next, chapter 6 examines another important influence at work here—the policy environment. This discussion highlights the ways in which this perception problem has often worked to impede the library community's ability to effectively engage in political discourse and policy making related to access to information.

Chapter Six

Information Policies Related to Human Rights and Social Justice

J. Taylor and Loeb (2014) have asserted that it is incumbent upon libraries to remind the public of the importance of free and open access to information. Librarians' adherence to this principle is firm, and yet they have often struggled to transform their ideological commitment into action. By presenting a number of key laws and policies related to information access to illustrate the different approaches that the library community has taken in response to the ever-changing legal and policy environment, this chapter will highlight the varying degrees of success libraries have had in their engagement. Before turning the discussion to specific laws and policies, however, it is necessary to provide a brief overview of the broader policy environment in which libraries operate. The position of public libraries within policy and politics in the United States is fully explored in *Public Libraries, Public Policies, and Political Processes: Serving and Transforming Communities in Times of Economic and Political Constraint* (Jaeger, Gorham, Bertot, & Sarin, 2014).

Here, we focus on how libraries, despite being local institutions, are increasingly impacted by policy making at the national level and on how the prevailing political and economic philosophies embraced by the federal government over the course of the second half of the twentieth century, together with libraries' traditional adherence to neutrality, have often precluded libraries from becoming effective participants in these national policy dialogues. To begin this policy discussion, it is important to pull together a number of threads that have already been introduced in this book.

Since the beginning of the modern public library movement in 1876, public libraries have viewed themselves as primarily local entities, based on local and state agencies providing the vast majority of funding and local level entities, like city councils and library boards, overseeing many of the operational decisions (Wiegand, 2011). Thus, for many years, local policies and politics most directly impacted libraries, often in terms of collection development, as well as library operations and funding. The impacts of state policies and politics have also been significant—while states are not generally a large source of funding, they have long maintained a role in standardizing and coordinating the public libraries in each state. In some states, virtually as soon as a library was built, representatives of the state voiced their opinions on the collections or the operations of the library (Wiegand, 2011).

As local and state government budgets have dwindled in the Great Recession, however, most public libraries, school libraries, and academic libraries at public universities have received proportionally decreased funding. The situation has been aggravated by the fact that many libraries rely on local property tax revenues for a large portion of their funding, and such revenues have fallen considerably in the wake of the collapse of the housing market. These reductions in funding adversely impact operating hours, collection development, resource acquisition, services, and staffing, all of which limit the ability of libraries to provide the level of service to the patrons that they both need and have come to expect.

While the past quarter century has seen greater attention paid to libraries at the national level (as discussed in greater detail in the later part of this chapter), an accompanying increase in federal funding to libraries has been noticeably absent. This absence is due largely to the dominance of a governing philosophy that emphasizes a smaller federal government and decreased support for public services (Fuller, 1994). Public libraries have suffered considerably in society as a result of the changes in political philosophy that were ushered in during the Reagan administration, leading to deregulation, changing tax and social priorities, spending cuts, and the emphasis on documentable contributions from organizations (Buschman, 2003). As discussed in chapter 2, the principles of neoliberal economic and neoconservative political ideologies work in tandem to undermine the value accorded to public goods and public services by demanding that public institutions—such as libraries and schools—demonstrate the economic contributions of the services they provide (Jaeger, Bertot, & Gorham, 2013; Jaeger, Gorham, Bertot, & Sarin, 2014). This philosophy places libraries in the near-impossible position of trying to place an economic value on knowledge and learning or on literacy and inclusion (Jaeger, Bertot, Kodama, Katz, & DeCoster, 2011; Jaeger, Taylor, Bertot, Perkins, & Wahl, 2012). In recent years, as governments at all levels have continued to reduce their overall spending in reaction to falling revenues, the struggle of libraries to define their value in economic terms has made them a particularly appealing target for additional spending reductions.

The current situation, as it has evolved since the start of the Great Recession, serves as a microcosm for the interrelationship between libraries that depend on public funding, policy making, and political processes. Politicians campaign on platforms that emphasize austerity and cost cutting and aggressively cut budgets of libraries and other institutions for the public good. All the while, earlier policy decisions that weakened the economy have led to an increasing number of people turning to libraries for help with finding a job, applying for social services, interacting with government agencies, and learning new digital skills through the technology access and assistance provided by the library, as well as availing themselves of entertainment options for which they can no longer afford to pay (Bertot, Jaeger, & Greene, 2013; Sigler et al., 2012; N. G. Taylor et al., 2012). Despite a growth in demand for their services, libraries are increasingly appearing in political debates as a symbol of big government by politicians who seek to curtail spending and/or limit social mobility of underrepresented populations (Bertot, Jaeger, & Sarin, 2012). And, notwithstanding the fact that the main economic arguments for austerity were based on poor assumptions with data, incorrect math, and data errors in spreadsheets that resulted in wildly incorrect results, these arguments continue to hold sway among conservative policy makers (Herndon, Ash, & Pollin, 2013). The end result is that, despite libraries increasingly taking on essential roles to ensure access to information and create digitally inclusive communities, library support at local, state, and federal levels continues to dwindle. Libraries, to date, have often failed to define these essential roles in a way that resonates with policy makers concerned primarily with the economic contributions of public services.

Further complicating matters are the library profession's long-standing efforts to act as impartial arbiters of information, often unhelpfully characterized as a position of neutrality. Neutrality manifests itself in two keys areas of librarianship: (1) trying to create collections that present as many different viewpoints as possible; and (2) trying to remain apolitical to the greatest extent possible. While both of these areas of neutrality are a source of controversy, the latter point is central to any discussion of the role of the library in policy making and political processes. This desire to remain apolitical is born, at least in part, out of a fear of getting involved in these processes. "We somehow seem to be a profession startled to find that we really do have deeply held convictions, that our words really do have meaning and consequence, and that when we act on our professional values someone actually notices" (Buschman, Rosenzweig, & Harger, 1994, p. 576).

Ultimately, libraries' attempts to remain apolitical are self-defeating, as their chosen stance has often relegated libraries to the sidelines in policy and political debates that affect their ability to function. In adopting this stance, the library has made it more difficult for its own perspective to be articulated and heard in political and policy-making processes over the years. The disengagement with the political process not only has consequences for libraries, it also limits the attention paid to library-generated perspectives on and solutions to issues of policy that would benefit other groups (Jaeger, Gorham, Sarin, & Bertot, 2013). One legal scholar recently labeled libraries as possessing "compelling answers" to current major policy problems, such as privacy and intellectual freedom, but bemoaned the disinclination of libraries to engage these issues in the policy and political arenas (N. M. Richards, 2013, p. 689).

Contemporary discourse surrounding these processes is dominated by the loudest voices and the most strident opinions. Librarians, who lack both of these attributes, are thus at a profound disadvantage vis-à-vis those espousing neoliberal economic and neoconservative political beliefs:

> By offering neutral responses in the increasingly partisan cultural atmosphere, the librarian denies him or herself the opportunity to definitely reverse the tide of negative educational trends which have seen the diminishment of the influence of the library in American society. . . . If the librarians cannot be motivated to take a stand on pressing social issues out of a sense of moral duty, certainly the librarians should break his or her neutrality in the name of self-interest. (Good, 2006–2007, p. 28)

The challenges presented by neutrality are reflected in the professional literature time and again as new social and political issues arise.

At various points in the last quarter century, arguments have been made for abandoning neutrality to promote educational equality, challenge antiterrorism laws, combat privatization, and advocate for multiculturalism, among many other issues (e.g., Berry & Rawlinson, 1991; Blanke, 1989; Durrani & Smallwood, 2006; Jerrard, Bolt, & Strege, 2012; Kniffel, 2002; Stoffle & Tarin, 1994). Moreover, across the Library Bill of Rights, the Code of Ethics, the ALA Policy Manual, and other ALA documents are many direct and indirect declarations of stances on political issues related to information, emphasizing themes related to freedom of expression, privacy, censorship, inclusion, and literacy. Over the years, some of these documents stray well beyond information issues, however, as evidenced by the inclusion of provisions related to issues such as pro-disarmament and pro-environmentalism in the ALA Policy Manual (2012a).

Despite these declarations, libraries have yet to abandon their long-standing stance of neutrality. The steadfastness of this stance, in combination with libraries' struggle to articulate their value in an environment increasingly hostile to the notion of public good, frequently places libraries in the position of having major political and policy decisions happen to them, with their voice basically unexpressed, unheard, or ignored (Jaeger & Bertot, 2011; Jaeger, Bertot, & Gorham, 2013). The gravity of this situation is highlighted when we consider how these very decisions shape funding, freedom of access to information, intellectual property, and library management, among many other core elements that determine the extent to which libraries can successfully serve—and promote rights and justice in—their communities.

The remainder of this chapter will focus on libraries' involvement in political discourse and policy making related to one of these core elements, namely, access to information. We have chosen to use access to information because, as previously noted, equity of access underlies most contributions that libraries can make to rights and justice. Given the breadth of policy issues that impact libraries' capacity to provide access to information, it is not surprising that there has been significant variation in both the nature and extent of the library community's engagement with these different issues. The library community's approaches to engagement run the gamut, from librarians inserting themselves into the epicenter of the legal action to remaining virtually silent as policy debates intensify around them. These different levels of engagement appear to reflect both varying levels of comfort with the issues and perceptions of the importance of different issues to libraries as institutions and/or the library profession.

To demonstrate the range of approaches to engagement undertaken by libraries, this chapter discusses laws and policies that both directly and indirectly challenge the ability of these institutions to provide open access to information. In every case, the lack of an organized and productive discourse has influenced the policy and legal outcomes. While there is some recognition that engagement in the political and policy processes is "a fundamental duty of all who believe in the very real contributions libraries make to U.S. culture, productivity, levels of literacy, and embodiment of democratic values" (Halsey, 2003, p. 1), the crisis mode in which libraries have been operating in recent years precludes them from presenting a unified voice in the political and policy debates that have far-reaching implications for their future. It should also be noted that, as a result of libraries and library professionals' reluctance to become directly engaged in political and policy-making processes, it has largely been left to a small number of professional organizations with limited lobbying arms—most notably ALA—to interject the perspectives of libraries into these debates. As highlighted throughout the remainder of this chapter, however, if a policy decision related to information access pits major technology corporations on one side and professional library organizations on the other, the practical advantages will not rest with the library organizations.

The ongoing debates about privatization, net neutrality, the FDLP, Internet filters, government surveillance of library activities, and copyright—notwithstanding key difference in the extent of the library community's involvement in these different issues—all highlight a central theme of this book, namely, how the evolving role of libraries, as well as the changing environments in which libraries exist, impact their ability to serve as vehicles for the promotion of human rights and social justice. The discourse has been different in each case, yet the inability of the library professionals to promote its position in a timely and effective manner is a common thread among them.

PRIVATIZATION

Privatization is perhaps one of the clearest examples of a policy that has potentially far-reaching implications for libraries as institutions. ALA defines privatization as "the shifting of library service from the public to the private sector through transference of library management and operations from a government agency to a commercial company" (ALA, 2011, p. 5). This action, of course, also threatens the continued ability of the library to operate in the public eye as a public institution providing open access to information. And, it is hard to imagine many corporations continuing human rights and social justice activities if they are not profitable.

The idea of privatization within the library context first emerged in the mid-1990s, largely as a cost-cutting measure championed by local government officials. The Riverside County Public Library System in California, for example, serving more than one million residents, was privatized in 1997. This approach did not garner universal acclaim, though, as evidenced by the fact that, at around the same time, the residents of Jersey City, New Jersey, protested to prevent the privatization of their library system (Hanley, 1998).

ALA's antiprivatization stance is well documented. In 2001, the ALA Council adopted the following policy statement with respect to privatization: "ALA affirms that publicly funded libraries should remain directly accountable to the public they serve. Therefore, the ALA opposes the shifting of policymaking and management oversight of library services for the public to the private for-profit sector" (ALA, 2001). A decade later, the 2010–2011 ALA Committee on Library Advocacy's Task Force on Privatization released a report that laid out the various issues involved in privatization, seeking to educate those within the library community about these issues so that they would be well prepared to engage in discussions related to library privatization within their communities. Central to the ALA's argument in this report is the conception of the library as foundational to democracy and critical to the public good and its role in connecting people, especially the "have-nots," with the information they need in order to participate in contemporary society. The report asserts that privatization—resulting in the community losing control over its library operations as well as its tax dollars—could have a range of adverse impacts on everything from quality of library services to governance to intellectual freedom. It suggests that private companies may not share libraries' commitment to protecting patron privacy or guaranteeing open access to information, thus couching at least part of their arguments in human rights language.

Fifteen years after privatization in libraries first came on the scene, however, it has yet to become a widespread phenomenon in the United States. At the time of the ALA Task Force report, twenty privatization contracts had been signed, and six of those had been either terminated or not renewed. Moreover, others have argued that ALA's conception of privatization is flawed and that what they actually are protesting is outsourcing. In fact, a 2000 study, funded by the ALA and conducted by the Texas Woman's University School of Library and Information Studies, sharply criticized the definition of privatization used by ALA. At the outset of their report, the researchers defined privatization differently—as "contracting out for services in a way that shifts control over policies for library collections and services from the public to the private sector"—but adopted the ALA Task Force's definition of outsourcing ("the contracting to external companies or organizations, functions that would otherwise be performed by library employees") (R. S. Martin, 2000, p. 4). After finding no instances of privatization (i.e., a library relinquishing control over policy to a vendor), the researchers shifted the focus of their study to the outsourcing of cataloging, selection, and management of library operations. Overall, the study found no evidence that outsourcing negatively impacts either library services or management. In particular, the study found "no evidence that outsourcing per se represents a threat to library governance, or to the role of the library in protecting the First Amendment rights of the public" (p. 53).

As evidenced by the task force's 2011 report and the recent publication of a book entitled *Privatizing Libraries* (Jerrard, Bolt, & Strege, 2012), which begins with a statement of the ALA's long-standing opposition to privatization, this study did little to encourage the ALA to modify their rhetoric or their policy stance. ALA has undoubtedly been instrumental in raising awareness about an issue that directly impacts libraries; however, by crafting a narrative that heavily uses the term "privatization" (rather than the less emotionally and politically charged term "outsourcing"), it has shaped the discourse in a way that tends to obscure the fact that we still know little about the ways in which changes in the management and operation of libraries actually impact the services they deliver to their users, including the human rights and social justice contributions made by libraries in their communities.

NET NEUTRALITY

As libraries increasingly embrace their role as the one place of free public Internet access and support within their communities, their commitment to providing open access to information has only grown stronger. As discussed below, the library community has often rallied against laws that operate to limit this access. Notwithstanding this commitment, for years, the library community has remained largely on the sidelines of the net neutrality debate. As defined by the ALA, net neutrality "is the concept of online non-discrimination. It is the principle that consumers/citizens should be free to get access to—or to provide—the Internet content and services they wish, and that consumer access should not be regulated based on the nature or source of that content or service" (ALA, 2014c, n.p.). Underlying the ALA's support for net neutrality is its commitment to freedom of expression and its belief in the potential for the Internet to promote intellectual diversity.

Until recently, however, the link between net neutrality and its importance to libraries was not a part of the debates waging between ISPs, telecommunications providers, human rights organizations, and other interested parties. The importance of net neutrality to libraries did not become part of the discourse until the U.S. Court of Appeals for the DC Circuit's ruling in *Verizon v. FCC* (2014), in which the court struck down key parts of the FCC's Open Internet Order, holding that the FCC overreached its authority in implementing net neutrality rules for broadband providers. Central to the court's finding of overreaching was the fact that the regulations at issue only applied to common carriers—the FCC's previous classification of broadband providers as information services thus precluded the application of these regulations to these providers.

Immediately following the *Verizon* ruling, the ALA, as well as the AALL and the Association of Research Libraries (ARL), came out with strongly worded statements, detailing the reasons for their opposition to this decision. The ALA statement brought to the forefront the issue of how net neutrality— or the lack thereof—directly impacts libraries:

> The court's decision gives commercial companies the astounding legal authority to block Internet traffic, give preferential treatment to certain Internet services or applications, and steer users to or away from certain web sites based on their own commercial interests. This ruling, if it stands, will adversely affect the daily lives of Americans and fundamentally change the open nature of the Internet, where uncensored access to information has been a hallmark of the communication medium since its inception. . . . Public libraries have become leading providers of public Internet access, providing service to millions of students, elderly citizens, people seeking employment and many others every single day. Approximately 77 million people use public library Internet access every year. These users of libraries' Internet services, and people all across the country, deserve equal access to online information and services. (ALA, 2014a, n.p.)

In February 2014, the FCC opened up a new rule-making docket to consider how it should proceed in light of the *Verizon* opinion and the ALA was one of the first to file a comment when this docket opened (L. Clarke, 2014).

The ALA, working with ARL and EDUCAUSE (a national nonprofit organization), reaffirmed its commitment to ensuring that the interests of public, school, and academic libraries remained part of the ongoing dialogue about net neutrality. Their comment also homed in on the connection between free and open access to information and the public good, arguing that the privileging of entertainment and commercial offerings over the online resources upon which students, researchers, and library patrons depend would create tiers of access. These tiers of access, in turn, would impede the ability of public institutions that foster learning, innovation, and research from continuing to play a vital role in the maintenance of a healthy society and economy.

Since that time, the ALA has indicated its commitment to remaining engaged in this matter. In an interview with the *Washington Post*, Lynne Bradley, the director of government relations at the ALA's Washington office, strongly affirmed libraries' and other public institutions' central role in maintaining equitable access to information, and provided some insight into the plans of the ALA and the greater library community to remain engaged in the debate on net neutrality:

> We'll participate in [FCC] proceedings in the coming months, pointing out the needs of library and our users as well as the unique role that public institutions in particular and education entities in general serve for the American public. We'll explain how we use the Internet and why the risk of being slowed down or, worse yet, being denied access is going to be a real problem for our institutions and for the people we serve. (Peterson, 2014, n.p.)

In July of 2014, the FCC released a Notice of Proposed Rulemaking, seeking to redress the untenable situation created by the *Verizon* decision, namely, the lack of legally enforceable rules to prevent broadband companies from engaging in practices that threaten Internet openness (FCC, 2014a). In connection with this notice, the FCC (2014a) specifically requested "comment on the role that the open Internet has for public institutions, such as public and school libraries, research libraries, and colleges and universities" as well as "on the impact of the openness of the Internet on free expression and civic engagement."

As the debates surrounding net neutrality escalated in the aftermath of the Verizon decision, the library community came together and began to articulate why it is crucial that their collective voice not be drowned out in these debates. With the February 2015 passage of new FCC net neutrality rules, it remains to be seen whether the ALA will, in fact, continue to interject itself into dialogues currently dominated by private interests. Regardless, the growing awareness within the library community of the connection between the issues surrounding net neutrality and the services and resources libraries provide is a definitive step in the right direction toward a greater understanding of the role that libraries are already playing in promoting human rights and social justice.

FEDERAL DEPOSITORY LIBRARY PROGRAM (FDLP)

The connection between information and democracy also underlies the ongoing discussions about the evolving role of the FDLP. The FDLP, administered by the Government Printing Office (GPO), was established to ensure that the public has access to information produced by the U.S. government. Such access, which is generally touted as one of the foundations of the American constitutional republic (Jaeger, Bertot, & Shuler, 2010), was originally achieved through the FDLP's geographic model of information access that used depository libraries throughout the country as the primary vehicles for distributing government information to citizens (Arrigo, 2004; Pettinato, 2007). The FDLP thus created "a secure, authentic, permanent network of local collections of government information, provided to the public without charge and preserved for the future" (J. A. Jacobs, Jacobs, & Yeo, 2005, p. 200).

The Government Printing Office Electronic Information Access Enhancement Act of 1993 (the GPO Access Act), requiring GPO to develop a more fully electronic depository program, ushered in a new era for the FDLP. Within the GPO itself, it led to a change in focus, from the production and dissemination of information to the provision of access to information. This dramatic shift in GPO's business focus caused both great excitement and upheaval among the federal depository community (Arrigo, 2004). From the outset of this change, the widespread availability of online government information called into question its traditional model of information access as well as the inherent value of the government documents held at FDLP member libraries (Jaeger, Bertot, & Shuler, 2010). The overhaul was relatively swift—approximately a decade after the passage of the GPO Access Act, 90 percent of the titles being delivered to FDLP libraries were made available electronically (Shuler, Jaeger, & Bertot, 2010).

In the wake of these technological developments, every library—and not just FDLP members—could serve as a public access point for government information. The reality that FDLP libraries were no longer the sole intermediaries between the public and government information became the center of the debate within the FDLP community (Jaeger, Bertot, & Shuler, 2010), as some questioned whether this development rendered the FDLP obsolete and others embraced this idea of an expanded universe of government information (Pettinato, 2007). The FDLP community did not respond in a cohesive manner, with some community members questioning the need to continue FDLP given the changing environment (J. A. Jacobs, Jacobs, & Yeo, 2005) and others contemplating leaving the program. Other FDLP libraries "began to rethink their activities and roles, with responses from the program's participants ranging from the development of public electronic gateways to a wide variety of government information sources, to the establishment of strategies and collaboration among libraries in a particular region to assure rapid information delivery" (Shuler, Jaeger, & Bertot, 2010, p. 12). And still others maintained that these technological developments did not, in fact, necessitate any change in approach on their parts.

There are a range of available approaches that libraries could promote in the policy debates to encourage others to see how these programs can continue to make valuable contributions in a changing environment (as discussed in Bertot, Jaeger, Shuler, Simmons, & Grimes, 2009; Jaeger, Bertot, & Shuler, 2010; Shuler, Jaeger, & Bertot, 2010), but the reaction in the field continues to be one of utter fragmentation, with Federal Depository Library Council (FDLC) meetings devolving into impasse and inaction. The lack of a cohesive response on the part of the FDLP libraries is troubling, given the fact that these developments do little to change the core mission of either GPO or the FDLP:

> All stakeholders share interrelated interests in ensuring that a national program of government information service meets the needs of citizens, communities, the nation as a whole, sustaining the civic conversation so necessary to the future health of our democracy. All these groups must work together to ensure that a FDLP's future organization supports the traditions of open access and permanence to government information, as well as citizen participation in a collaborative, Internet-enabled service environment. (Jaeger, Bertot, & Shuler, 2010, p. 476)

Acknowledgment of the changes that have been occurring over the past twenty years (resulting in a focus on public service, rather than physical collections), together with some level of consensus to guide the way forward, is crucial (Shuler, Jaeger, & Bertot, 2010, p. 14). The alternative—increasing fragmentation—will inevitably lead to a policy solution that does not effectively meet the needs of the FDLP libraries or their patrons. As providing access to government information and services—and the technical skills to use them—is a particularly important contribution of libraries to human rights and social justice, this policy issue has significant implications for all types of libraries.

CHILDREN'S INTERNET PROTECTION ACT (CIPA)

In the case of CIPA and its predecessors, libraries became vocal advocates for their patrons' First Amendment rights, challenging repeated attempts by Congress to address the issue of pornographic and other types of online content deemed to be indecent under the law. Pursuant to CIPA, any public library receiving "universal service" (E-rate) discounts (established by the Telecommunications Act of 1996 [P.L. 104–104]) or Library Services and Technology Act (LSTA) grants from the Institute for Museum and Library Services (IMLS) to state library agencies was required to install filters on networked computers so as to prevent children from viewing certain categories of regulated online content. "Using congressional authority under the spending clause of Article I, section 8 of the Constitution, CIPA ties the direct or indirect receipt of certain types of federal funds to the installation of filters on library and school computers" (Jaeger & Yan, 2009, p. 7).

Since their inception, both E-rate discounts and LSTA grants made significant contributions to the rise in the availability of free public Internet access in libraries (Jaeger & McClure, 2004). In particular, when CIPA was passed, many libraries relied on E-rate funds to support library technology and Internet access, leading them to feel as if they had no choice but to remain in compliance with CIPA. Libraries were thus put into a very difficult position—they do not create the online content that CIPA seeks to regulate, but they nevertheless became a target in the federal government's effort to protect children from it. As a result, libraries found themselves juggling several different legitimate interests, namely, their need for federal funding, their commitment to providing unrestricted access to information, and their desire to limit children's exposure to potentially harmful content.

Challenges to CIPA were based on various grounds—the filtering mechanisms were severely flawed; the mechanisms set forth in the law for adult patrons to obtain unfiltered access were cumbersome and librarians could exercise discretion in using them; and the statutory requirements were far more broad than they needed to be, covering all patrons and staff, regardless of their age (Gathegi, 2005; Jaeger, Bertot, & McClure, 2004; Jaeger & McClure, 2004; Jaeger, McClure, Bertot, et al., 2005; Jaeger & Yan, 2009). In January 2001, a group of libraries, library associations (including the ALA), library patrons, and website publishers filed suit against the federal government in the U.S. District Court for the Eastern District of Pennsylvania, challenging CIPA on its face. The district court ruled in favor of the ALA, finding that CIPA was facially unconstitutional because it required public libraries to block a substantial amount of constitutionally protected speech, thereby violating the First Amendment.

The case was appealed to the United States Supreme Court, and the district court's opinion was overturned. The court ruled that CIPA neither violated the free speech clause of the First Amendment, nor imposed an impermissible condition on public libraries, concluding "that the federal assistance to libraries was meant to assist the libraries in its traditional role of obtaining appropriate educational and informational material, and Congress could demand that the funds be used only for that purpose" (Gathegi, 2005, p. 11). Perhaps most disheartening is that the Supreme Court's ruling revealed an utter lack of understanding of the goals of libraries and the contributions of libraries to their communities (Gathegi, 2005; Jaeger, Bertot, & McClure, 2004). This was made clear, for example, by the court's agreement with Congress's characterization of the Internet as "no more than a technological extension of the book stack."

In the aftermath of the CIPA ruling, commentators within the library community made several observations that remain relevant today. First, CIPA aptly illustrated the consequences of implementing information policies without giving due regard during the development of the legislation to the impacts of these policies on individuals, institutions, and society as a whole (Jaeger & Yan, 2009). Second, the CIPA ruling was limited to the extent that the court only found that the text of the law, as written, did not clearly infringe on freedom of speech. This ruling, however, did not address the application of the law in public and school libraries, leaving open the door to as-applied challenges in the future (Jaeger, Bertot, & McClure, 2004). There were many potential grounds for further legal challenges to the constitutionality of the application of CIPA, all of which related "to the fact that CIPA could significantly reduce the amount of free speech that adult patrons could access through the Internet in public libraries" (Jaeger & McClure, 2004, n.p.). Subsequent research about the impacts of CIPA have found that the requirements of the law significantly negatively affect the ability of patrons to meet their information needs due to the overblocking of content and the ability of librarians to promote digital literacy and digital inclusion (Batch, 2014). The most disproportionate impacts are on the sixty million children and adults who lack access to the Internet outside of the library (Batch, 2014).

The Supreme Court's ruling in CIPA thus raises the question of whether a different outcome could have been attained had the ALA taken a different approach—that is, waited until the law could be challenged as applied rather than challenging the law on its face. Ten years later, this ill-fated challenge still provides a cautionary tale of what can go wrong when the library community chooses to become embroiled in legal and policy issues. In hindsight, a more robust policy and politics discourse—one embracing their human rights and social justice roles—in the field would have better prepared librarians to advocate for a different approach in the law while it was being written and enabled them to develop a strategy for challenging the law if and when such action was deemed necessary.

USA PATRIOT ACT

The post-9/11 period gave rise to laws like the USA PATRIOT Act and the Homeland Security Act, which enhanced government agencies' ability to collect a wide range of libraries' physical and electronic records and to observe patron behaviors in libraries, while also limiting the government information available through use of overzealous classification standards and permitting information to be removed from library collections (Jaeger, Bertot, & McClure, 2003; Jaeger & Burnett, 2005; Jaeger, McClure, Bertot, & Snead, 2004). To librarians, the government's heightened authority in this area was in direct conflict with their ethical standards and, specifically, their commitment to protecting the confidentiality of patrons' reading habits, research behaviors, and other information seeking behaviors (Klinefelter, 2003).

Among the provisions of the USA PATRIOT Act that have been scrutinized closely by the library community are (1) Section 505, which introduced significant changes to several existing laws regarding the use of national security letters (NSLs) by the FBI to "seek customer and consumer transaction information in national security investigations from communications providers, financial institutions and credit agencies" and (2) Section 215, which allows easier access to books, records, documents, and other items sought in connection with a terror investigation. Much of the opposition to these provisions focused on how they expanded the authority of the government to investigate the ordinary, everyday activity of citizens by relaxing the standards governing the government's exercise of this authority, while prohibiting those who received an NSL or Section 215 order from disclosing this fact. Taken together, these and other USA PATRIOT Act provisions set the stage for collections of large quantities of information from libraries (Jaeger, Bertot, McClure, & Langa, 2006).

Librarians also expressed concern about the "chilling effect" that the exercise of these expanded powers could have on patrons' use of libraries: "Librarians want library records kept private because they fear misinterpretation of reading choices and the effect that searches have on readers. . . .Their records are 'not ordinary third-party records like telephone or bank records. They should not be available to intelligence agencies just for the asking'" (K. Martin, 2002, p. 290). This so-called chilling effect implicates patrons' First Amendment rights to the extent that the Supreme Court's conception of free speech includes the right to receive free speech (K. Martin, 2002). Several years after passage of the law, Jaeger and Burnett (2005) observed that the USA PATRIOT Act continued to cause unrest among members of the library community, particularly when they were pulled into a law enforcement investigation. Due to their unease over the new responsibilities foisted upon them by the USA PATRIOT Act, many librarians became actively involved in efforts to modify the USA PATRIOT Act so as to mitigate its impacts on libraries and their patrons.

The quick and impassioned response of the library community to the USA PATRIOT Act was due, at least in part, to the fact that they had fought similar battles in the past. In the 1960s, the FBI launched the LAP, targeting libraries that served communities with high populations of immigrant, intellectual, or liberal residents in an attempt to discover any reading habits of library patrons that might be cause for security concern. Focused particularly on Soviet activities, the FBI sought the assistance of librarians in these institutions to obtain confidential patron information (Doyle, 2005). This program, which continued through the 1980s, was a major driving force behind efforts by librarians and library associations to enact state laws to safeguard the confidentiality of library records and library use (Klinefelter, 2003). Therefore, at the time that the USA PATRIOT Act was passed, individuals in many states had a legally recognized privacy interest in their library records. The USA PATRIOT Act, however, created a seismic shift in the always shaky balance between national security and individual liberty (Jaeger, Bertot, & McClure, 2003), and the potentially far-reaching implications of this law led to a wide range of responses within the library community. In voicing opposition to this law many librarians once again cast themselves in the role of defender of their patrons' rights of privacy and freedom of expression. The ALA's Resolution on the USA PATRIOT Act and Related Measures That Infringe on the Rights of Library Users, for example: "urge[d] the United States Congress to: 1. provide active oversight to the implementation of the USA PATRIOT Act and other related measures . . . and 3. amend or change the sections of these laws and the guidelines that threaten or abridge the rights of inquiry and free expression" (ALA, 2003, n.p.).

As with the LAP, librarians were forced to reevaluate how they handle patron information, leading them to conduct privacy audits and develop practices to reduce the collection of personally identifying information (Klinefelter, 2007). Much of the professional discourse in the immediate post-9/11 period thus focused on resistance to the law—advocating for wholesale shredding of physical records and deleting of electronic records, computer usage information, and patron checkout records—with some even advocating that librarians should be willing to go to jail to oppose the law. Librarians' activities—which also included hosting panel discussions, promoting association standards for privacy, and posting privacy policies—created buzz within the media, and librarians' objections to the USA PATRIOT Act were extensively covered (Klinefelter, 2003). Having thrust themselves into the middle of the post-9/11 debate about the appropriate balance between national security and individual liberty, librarians then had to grapple with the uncomfortable glare of the political spotlight, as the attorney general of the United States questioned their patriotism for objecting to the intrusive and extensive nature of these laws, even attacking them for spreading "breathless reports and baseless hysteria" (Klinefelter, 2003, p. 222).

Librarians also found themselves at the center of lengthy legal proceedings in *Doe v. Gonzalez*. In that case, a consortium of Connecticut libraries filed suit against the federal government after receiving an NSL demanding all information associated with a particular computer over a given period of time. Here, First Amendment issues took center stage, with the plaintiffs, requesting an injunction to lift the nondisclosure provision so that the librarian who received the NSL request could participate in public debate about the reauthorization of the USA PATRIOT Act. The district court granted the injunction, finding that the act's nondisclosure provision violated the First Amendment.

As this case was winding its way through the court system, the reauthorization of the USA PATRIOT Act became a subject of intense discussion. Section 505 and other provisions were initially set to expire on December 31, 2005. The 2005 Reauthorization Act made Section 218 permanent, placed four-year sunsets on Sections 206 and 205, while imposing some limitations on the government's power in these areas (e.g., increased congressional and judicial oversight), and amended Section 505 to, among other things, clarify the availability of judicial review of both NSL requests and the disclosure requirements. Despite opposition from within Congress, Section 215 was extended several times, most recently extended in May 2011 for an additional four years. Subsequent attempts within Congress to reform the NSL process, including the USA PATRIOT Act Amendments Act of 2009 and the Judicious Use of Surveillance Tools in Counterterrorism Efforts Act of 2010, were unsuccessful.

In the years since the initial frenzy caused by the USA PATRIOT Act, the debates surrounding it have understandably dwindled but, from time to time, they have been reignited. In 2007, for example, Section 505 came under attack after a report prepared by the FBI's Office of the Inspector General revealed a dramatic increase in the number of NSL requests, from 8,500 in the year before the USA PATRIOT Act was passed to 143,074 between 2003 and 2005. The report also detailed a number of instances of improper or illegal issuance and use of NSLs, including failures to obtain necessary approvals and the unauthorized collection of information.

In recent years, there has been a decline in the number of NSLs from 24,827 requests concerning 14,212 U.S. persons in 2010 to 16,511 requests concerning 7,201 persons in 2011. Notwithstanding this decline, the issues raised by the USA PATRIOT Act—as discussed in Gorham-Oscilowski & Jaeger, 2008; Jaeger, Bertot, & McClure, 2003; Jaeger & Burnett, 2005; Jaeger, McClure, Bertot, & Snead, 2004—remain significant today. The discourse has often suffered, however, from the lack of a sufficient connection between libraries' initial strong reaction to the USA PATRIOT Act and the law's actual impact on library services and/or library use. While data was initially difficult to collect due to the act's nondisclosure requirements (Albitz, 2005), the removal of these requirements did not pave the way for a clearer understanding of how much has changed in the post-9/11 period. And, while the Justice Department stated in 2005 that Section 215 had yet to be used to acquire library records (Doyle, 2005) and some within the library community have questioned the actual impact of this provision (Martins & Martins, 2005; Shaffer, 2014), *Doe v. Gonzalez* confirms that NSLs have been issued to libraries. Moreover, in a 2007 resolution, the ALA noted that "FBI Director Robert Mueller caused classified written testimony to be provided to the Senate Judiciary Committee on March 30, 2007, concerning other instances when FBI agents may have used NSLs to obtain information from libraries about library users" (ALA, 2007, n.p.).

The secretive nature of these surveillance activities, despite the removal of nondisclosure requirements, makes it nearly impossible to assess how often and under what circumstances the government is engaging in these activities. Nor do we have a clear understanding as to whether in the aftermath of the USA PATRIOT Act, patrons have limited use of libraries as a means to protect their privacy. Perhaps due to this lack of knowledge of the act's actual impacts, the vehemently negative initial reaction to it a decade ago has been replaced by an apparent lack of meaningful discussion about it. In 2003, Klinefelter maintained that "the idea of privacy in using a library is now a touchstone for debate about how to achieve a balance between security and privacy in the post–September 11 world" (p. 226). A little over a decade later, it is debatable whether that remains true, even though the issues raised by the USA PATRIOT Act have tremendous implications for the information access that underlies so many human rights and social justice roles of libraries.

COPYRIGHT

Libraries operate as a balancing force between the interests of copyright owners and copyright users, by virtue of the limitations placed on the former by Sections 107 (fair use) and 108 (reproduction by libraries and archives) of the Copyright Act. As the Digital Millennium Copyright Act (DMCA) and other recent copyright reforms have sought to shift this balance in favor of copyright owners, libraries are struggling to understand how these reforms alter their legal rights and responsibilities in an increasingly digital environment (Butler, 2003; Travis, 2006). Extensions of copyright protection to such incredible lengths—life of the author plus eighty years—create many questions of ownership, and these extensions create significant tensions with the increases in access to information brought about by the Internet and electronic files. Digital copies of orphan works—older works where the copyright owner is untraceable—became virtually unusable, even by the libraries that own the items (Brito and Dooling, 2006; Carlson, 2005).

In 2011, the Library Copyright Alliance, comprised of the ALA, the ACRL, and the ARL, issued a statement that addressed these increasingly complex copyright issues, acknowledging that the divergence of stakeholders' interests and certain stakeholders' reluctance to alter the status quo made it difficult to attain consensus. This statement called for reforms that would encourage libraries to make appropriate fair use of copyrighted materials by eliminating the possibility of statutory damages, so as to encourage "library-initiated projects involving mass digitization, the use of orphan works, and large-scale preservation" (Library Copyright Alliance, 2006, n.p.).

The balance was poised to undergo yet another radical shift in 2012, with the introduction of SOPA. SOPA was strongly supported by content creators, such as the movie, television, and music industries, and it was strongly opposed by the content providers, including the large Internet companies. The proposed legislation would have benefited content creators by giving them the right to shut down any website deemed to have facilitated copyright or trademark infringement before any such infringement is proven, thereby prioritizing the rights of one stakeholder entirely over another. During the intense debates surrounding this legislation, however, the library community's response was rather muted. The ALA and other library associations, including the AALL, urged their members to contact their elected officials and urge them to vote "no" on SOPA but this issue failed to grab the attention of the larger library community in a meaningful way. This lack of discourse is somewhat surprising—as asserted by the AALL, SOPA threatened free speech by chilling users' willingness to use copyrighted works, as well as orphan works.

Notwithstanding the fact that SOPA, which was ultimately withdrawn from consideration in Congress, had potentially far-reaching implications for open access to online information, the potential impact of this legislation on libraries never became a meaningful part of the discourse. As evidenced by the formation of the Library Copyright Alliance, the library community is aware of the myriad issues surrounding copyright reform and has had a degree of success in interjecting its views into policy debates that directly impact libraries. As its limited engagement with respect to SOPA demonstrates, however, it has been less successful in doing so in those debates that involve issues with indirect—yet still significant—impacts on libraries.

RIGHTS AND JUSTICE IN DEBATES OF POLICY AND POLITICS

All these examples show a clear failure of the library community to carve out a meaningful and well-thought-out role in ongoing policy debates, a fact that has potentially far-reaching implications. The end result is that, by and large, library professionals, educators, and researchers have not been extremely successful in engaging in this arena, rendering them unable or unwilling to articulate their human rights and social justice roles to policymakers and politicians and the impacts of political and policy decisions on these roles. The laws and policies discussed here demonstrate that there is no single reason for libraries' lack of success but that, in each case, there was a confluence of factors that inhibited them from engaging in a productive manner from the outset. The library community's disorganized and counterproductive response in some cases, and lack of awareness of key issues in other cases, has all too frequently led to the institution of a law or policy that ultimately limits the ability of libraries to guarantee access and equity, as well as other key elements of their human rights and social justice roles.

One reason for the lack of success is that the purpose of the library as an institution of social justice and human rights is present in day-to-day actions, but not in formal rhetoric. It is harder to justify the expenditure of resources on indirect issues when there is a lack of clarity in an institution's purpose. The lack of a focus on the human rights and social justice roles in library advocacy also robs libraries of a unifying narrative of their contributions to society and the ways in which they could best be supported by policy decisions. One area that the library community desperately needs to address is the best way to own its roles in ensuring rights and justice and the most effective ways in which to engage the policy and political processes with this clear and central purpose.

Chapter Seven

Arsenals of Human Rights and Social Justice

When Richard Nixon gave his first speech as president during his inauguration in 1969, he emphasized the need for peaceful dialogue rather than agitation, partisanship, or violent confrontation to solve the social problems in the United States. While subsequent events would demonstrate that virtually every statement he made in the speech about what he wanted to do as president was not true, one section was primarily true—a long list he presented of the problems confronting the nation (Perlstein, 2008). As he assumed the presidency, social upheaval had become a defining characteristic of the time: inner-city riots; antiwar protests; assassinations of political leaders; campus takeovers; mass shootings; black power, white power, and Cuban power movements; the domestic terrorism of the Weathermen; the stoning of American embassies abroad; the anarchy of the Yippies; and the radicalization of feminism; among much else. In one section of the speech, Nixon rattled through a list of all of these problems, and amid all of these things that were really happening, he tossed in a reference to the burning of libraries.

For all of the social unrest of the late 1960s, the United States did not experience a rash of library burnings. Yet, Nixon used the reference to this nonexistent problem to add emotional heft to his list of real problems. If libraries are being burned, the message implied, then all hope for our society might be lost. Such is the power of libraries—and visceral impact as central to community—that Nixon felt the need to conjure a threat to libraries to add gravity to what was already a monumental set of social problems.

As obvious as it may seem, remembering that libraries do not exist in a vacuum when they try to help their communities is extremely important. The larger social and policy environment has direct influence on libraries' abilities to effect change, as well as the way in which they are perceived. In this case, Nixon played on the emotional resonance of libraries to bring the threats of society closer to home—you might not live near an inner city, but you certainly live near a library, and the dirty hippies or scary poor people might be trying to take it away from you. This clause about library burning may in fact be Nixon's first bit of fear mongering as president, a tool that would come to define his years in office.

Of course, far less histrionic and hysterical figures than Richard Nixon have used the image of libraries for gain in many different ways since the beginning of the modern library movement in the mid-1800s. The battles over the ways in which libraries are governed and the ways in which libraries are perceived, however, have evolved significantly in that time. The main difference can be found in the move from tangible resources to intangible ones.

In the pre-Internet years, the library could more readily demonstrate a clear contribution to communities. The programs to help community members have been ongoing for more than a century, but unless you attend the programs or happen to be in the library when they occur, you would not know they were there. Individual help is even harder to document. But books, periodicals, and other tangible items were used to provide the physical evidence—and source of community pride—in support of the library's standing and its contributions to the community and to larger democratic ideals. As public and school libraries were founded in the 1800s and early 1900s, local governments began to boast about the number of volumes in their local library collections as a point of civic pride (Wiegand, 2011).

Now, even the resources that patrons rely on are primarily intangible, so the increased contributions to individuals and communities have become even harder to see from the outside. Though the previous chapters have provided a large number of unique contributions to the lives of individuals and entire communities, the contributions of libraries are more abstract, moving from a repository model to an educational and social services model. What libraries do now is more vital to their communities than at any previous time, as they provide the intellectual tools and infrastructure of democracy while also being the central point of access, literacy, and inclusion in the information environment for communities.

JUSTIFYING LIBRARIES

The impact of this change on the perceptions of libraries has been significant. A national survey by the Pew Internet & the American Life project in January 2013 demonstrates the depth of attachment that the members of the public have for their public libraries. Among Americans age sixteen and older, an astounding 91 percent believe that public libraries are important to their communities and 76 percent say public libraries are important to their families (Zickuhr, Rainie, & Purcell, 2013). This finding echoes another recent study that found that 71 percent of citizens say public libraries spend their money well and that 52 percent of citizens favor tax increases if their local libraries need additional support (Wooden, 2006). However, in the 2013 study, only 22 percent of respondents were familiar with most or all of the services offered by their public library (Zickuhr, Rainie, & Purcell, 2013). Therein lies the problem for all types of libraries: other than the direct beneficiaries of the community goods that they provide, these contributions are primarily unnoticed. This leaves the majority of society with a vague or outdated notion of the contributions of libraries. Unfortunately, "the value of a good library—like good teaching—is extraordinarily difficult to quantify" (Buschman, 2005, p. 1). The impact of failing to articulate these roles can leave them ignored in policy-making circles. A 2014 report from the Aspen Institute (Garmer, 2014)—an organization that carries considerable influence with policy makers—on the future of public libraries does not mention the terms "human rights" or "social justice" once in the eighty-page report.

The struggle to justify the existence of libraries and to demonstrate contributions have been themes throughout the modern era of librarianship, and a brief review of library history is useful to demonstrate this struggle. When public libraries, school libraries, and public schools were first being established around the country in the mid-1800s, the primary beneficiaries were the elite families in the community who were literate, had leisure time, and could afford to allow their children to attend school rather than work; education of the working classes was a secondary benefit (Borden, 1931; Pungitore, 1995). The books in these early public and school libraries focused on the information needs and values of one specific community group and included dictionaries, grammars, books on political and moral issues, as well as books on practical sciences like agriculture, anatomy, astronomy, biology, chemistry, geometry, and mathematics (DuMont, 1977). The "felt cultural superiority of librarians led them to a concept of the library as a sort of benevolent school of social ethics" (Garrison, 1993, p. 40). During the period of prescriptive roles for libraries, leaders of the library profession were greatly opposed to social change and feared the labor rights movement and other forces reshaping American society (Garrison, 1993; Lerner, 2009; McCrossen, 2006; Preer, 2008).

At the first ALA meeting in 1876, "most agreed that the mass reading public was generally incapable of choosing its own reading materials judiciously" (Wiegand, 1986, p. 10). Civic and political leaders believed that libraries could provide a civilizing influence on the masses and be a means to shape the populace into adhering to hegemonic social norms (Augst, 2001; Garrison, 1993; Harris, 1973, 1976). This attitude was reflected in the elitist and paternalistic attitudes of most public libraries in selecting materials for the public betterment and in attempting to be social stewards of the general population (Augst, 2001; Heckart, 1991; Wiegand, 1986).

These attitudes changed quickly, however, as all of the innovations in public service around the time of the First World War and subsequent influx of immigrants occurred, as detailed in chapter 2. By the 1930s, libraries more firmly began to turn away from their previous roles as agents of social control. In reaction to the Second World War, libraries created and adopted a new primary social role as the veritable marketplace of ideas, offering materials that represented a diversity of views and interests, while opposing censorship and other social controls (Geller, 1974; Heckart, 1991). Numerous factors affected this reorientation, but a key change was the effect Fascist governments were having on public access to information in many parts of the world in the late 1930s, specifically through lethal suppression of expression, closing of libraries, and public book burnings (Geller, 1984; Robbins, 1996; Stielow, 2001).

After World War II, American libraries were so secure in their role in working with various community groups and promoting democracy—through supporting continuing education, serving the information needs of poor and recent immigrants, having special events for children, providing education to the working classes, opening branch libraries, and other forms of service—that a major history written at the time was proudly titled *Arsenals of a Democratic Culture* (Ditzion, 1947). Public libraries actively participated in voter registration and participation drives to increase voter turnout in the 1952 presidential election, firmly establishing the modern concept of the public library as a reliable "community source for serious, nonpartisan information on a central issue of the day" (Preer, 2008, p. 19).

These increasing commitments to their communities coincided with, and were likely fueled by, a time of robust increases in economic support of public libraries by local communities. The post–World War II economic boom that continued into the 1960s led to communities passing sales taxes, property taxes, and local income taxes as means to support public library expansion (Chatters, 1957). In fact, between 1936 and 1955, funding for libraries in the seventy-six largest cities in the United States grew at a rate far greater than rates of growth for total city expenditures (Chatters, 1957). Libraries also began to better serve larger communities by integrating into city- and county-level public library systems in many places (Leigh, 1957).

The path to a professional commitment to serving communities was not always smooth, however. Even after the passage of the Library Bill of Rights in 1939, many public libraries still banned John Steinbeck's *The Grapes of Wrath* for its political views (Samek, 2001). Other major writers that there were contemporaneous attempts to censor in libraries included Theodore Dreiser, Warwick Deeping, George Eliot, Thomas Hardy, Nathaniel Hawthorne, and Sinclair Lewis (Berninghausen, 1948a, 1948b). In the 1940s and

1950s, some public libraries were still uncomfortable with the idea of equal access to all, while, in sharp contrast, others took a clear lead in the civil rights movement (Robbins, 2000, 2007). The decision across the profession to actively support access in the face of attempts to censor collections at the local and broader levels has come to define the commitment of libraries to standing up for the needs of their communities. Nevertheless, the collections of many libraries were directly and indirectly influenced by the politics of the McCarthy era, often leading to the silencing of unpopular viewpoints in many library collections (Jaeger & Burnett, 2005; P. S. Richards, 2001).

Thus, between the middle of the 1800s and the middle of the 1900s, libraries moved through several major different perceptions of themselves (Jaeger, Sarin, Gorham, & Bertot, 2013). They began as a promoter of upper-class values and determiner of the readings habits of the masses, and then became an institution focused on the mainstream of society. At a fairly brisk pace, the inclusiveness was expanded to most of the community, including new arrivals. By the 1950s, they had matured into an institution fighting for specific principles, including openness to all viewpoints and inclusive communities, which has primarily continued to this day. That is a rather spectacular series of transformations in the ways that libraries presented themselves as important to society.

These shifts in justifications for support and demonstration of value have reflected the changes in libraries themselves and the changes in society that libraries were reacting to and trying to support. They also have reflected an increasing level of government interest in intervening in the activities of libraries (Jaeger, Sarin, Gorham, & Bertot, 2013). In spite of different social pressures, major technological change, and increasing political intervention, libraries have spent the past century continually refining their roles as institutions of rights and justice in their communities. But they have not been particularly good about explaining or demonstrating these roles, hence the current confusion by many community members, including many library users, of the actual range of contributions that libraries make to their communities. Fortunately, there are data that can be employed to explain and demonstrate this range of essential contributions of libraries to access education, inclusion, rights, and justice.

DEMONSTRATING SUPPORT FOR RIGHTS AND JUSTICE

Libraries of all types have long been focused on articulating their value to their communities, relying on assertions of value related to ideals; much less frequently do libraries use data to demonstrate their value to community through concrete numbers (Jaeger, Bertot, Kodama, Katz, & DeCoster, 2011; Jaeger, Gorham, Sarin, & Bertot, 2013). The approach of value demonstration through data has the ability to help overcome the previously noted lack of understanding of the full range of library contributions and intangible nature of so much of what they do now. A value demonstration approach would also allow greater opportunities to connect libraries' activities to the language and structure of human rights and social justice beyond the walls of the library.

A recent national survey of the digital literacy and digital inclusion activities of public libraries provides an example of this opportunity to use data to better explain the ways in which libraries contribute. The 2014 Libraries and Digital Inclusion survey was designed as a new generation of the Public Libraries and the Internet studies that were conducted for twenty years (Bertot, Jaeger, et al., 2014). The study now has a specific focus on digital literacy and digital inclusion because of their centrality in the ways that public libraries now serve their communities when so much of civic, social, educational, and professional life is centered online. The results of the survey emphatically demonstrate the roles of libraries and the technology access and education that they provide in supporting human rights and social justice in their communities.

Key findings from the survey include:

- All public libraries (100 percent) provide free public Internet access.
- All public libraries (100 percent) provide free access to online educational databases.
- Almost all public libraries (96.5 percent) provide homework assistance.
- Digital reference services are available in 91.5 percent of public libraries.
- Most libraries (89.5 percent) provide access to e-books.
- A majority of libraries (55.1 percent) offer online language learning courses and tools.
- A majority of libraries (53.3 percent) offer work spaces for mobile workers.
- The average public library outlet has twenty Internet-enabled workstations. (Bertot, Jaeger, et al., 2014)

All of these elements of the hardware, software, and educational infrastructure at public libraries support their roles as institutions of human rights and social justice. The provision of all of these services and resources for free makes it possible for many members of their communities to be included and have equal opportunities in terms of information, communication, education, employment, social support, health, and myriad other rights under the UDHR. In some communities the needs for the services listed above are quite pronounced. In Miami, Florida, for example, 48 percent of students have no home access to the Internet, but all of the students in public schools need to use computers and Internet for doing and submitting homework, overwhelming public library hours, space, and resources as a result (Hanks, 2014; *Miami Herald*, 2014).

The results of the survey also demonstrate that these contributions to human rights and social justice extend far beyond the infrastructure and space of public libraries. The educational roles of public librarians actively expand their roles in human rights and social justice:

- Education and learning programs—including basic literacy, digital literacy, summer reading, continuing education, foreign language instruction, and maker spaces—are offered in 99.5 percent of public libraries.
- Technology training is provided in 98 percent of public libraries.
- Employment resource training, assistance, and programs are available in 95 percent of public libraries.
- Community, civic engagement, and e-government training, assistance, and programs are available in 75 percent of public libraries.
- Health and wellness programs are offered by 57.9 percent of public libraries.
- Assistance in finding and assessing health insurance plans are even available in 37.3 percent of public libraries. (Bertot, Jaeger, et al., 2014)

Without public libraries addressing these needs, many members of their communities would be left with limited or no access and education in all of these areas that are vital to being an informed, included, and equal member of the community. Through the findings of this survey, public libraries both facilitate rights and justice, such as teaching digital literacy skills and providing free Internet access, and provide support for rights and justice in other contexts, such as using the literacy and access tools to find employment and participate civically. Data like these effectively and emphatically demonstrate that libraries—in this case public libraries—are human rights and social justice institutions. Having the data by which to articulate the human rights and social justice roles of libraries is not sufficient, however, as librarians have to commit to advocating based on these roles that have become so central to libraries.

A DWELLER ON THE THRESHOLD

As has been noted repeatedly in this book, libraries engage in the activities of human rights and social justice on a daily basis—it is the essence of what they are and what they do. A library is the "actions, interactions, and transformations that its existence makes possible, every day, for people from all walks of life" (Hummel, 2012, p. 4). Yet, they have not generally placed themselves within the context or language of human rights and social justice.

They are an institution of human rights and social justice and they support the activities of other institutions of human rights and social justice, but they have been hesitant to label themselves as such. This makes the field of librarianship seem to be a dweller on the threshold, standing at the door of human rights and social justice, but not quite willing to commit to describing itself in these terms or admit the importance of what it already does.

The reason for this confused and counterproductive position is heavily rooted in the traditional fear of the field in taking obvious political stances. As discussed in chapter 6, libraries have a history of trying to remain apolitical to the greatest extent possible. Some librarians present a neutral—that is, apolitical—posture as an act of service to patrons, while others see the commitment to a plurality of opinions in library collections as mitigating against political engagement by the field (Byrne, 2003; McMenemy, 2007).

Neutrality, though, is an unrealistic ideal that relies on the nonexistent opinion-free librarian selecting nonexistent bias-free materials (Alfino & Pierce, 2001; Budd, 2006; Burton, 2009; Samek, 2001; Wiegand, 2011). Critics of neutrality have noted a huge range of additional flaws in the position (Burton, 2009; Cornelius, 2004; Durrani & Smallwood, 2006; Floridi, 2002; J. B. Graham, 2003; Shavit, 1986). As a practical matter, proclamations of neutrality are not truly representative of the reality of the activities of the library profession. The ALA has adopted policy stances on political issues related to information, such as privacy, as well as issues that do not appear to have any direct connection to information, such as disarmament (Jaeger, Gorham, Bertot, & Sarin, 2014).

In the context of human rights and social justice, neutrality is particularly pernicious, as the drive to be seen as apolitical means that the impact of all of the human rights and social justice work—which are inherently political acts promoting inclusion and equality—are hidden or labeled something else to avoid accusations within the field of failing to be neutral. Some actions of human rights and social justice that are common among libraries, however, fly in the face of any attempt by libraries to remain neutral. Consider the context of teaching digital literacy:

- Materials of all types—including everything online—are not neutral and, as educators, librarians must make patrons aware of this reality (Alfino & Pierce, 2001; Budd, 2006; Burton, 2009);
- Teaching people to be able to evaluate among the potential information sources online is impossible if the librarian maintains a stance of neutrality pretending that some sources are not more accurate or reliable than others (J. B. Graham, 2003; Jaeger, Bertot, Thompson, Katz, & DeCoster, 2012);
- Presenting all sides of an issue as having equal moral weight is engaging in moral relativism and misleading patrons, particularly when they are

searching through the great many sources of varying quality and authority online (Good, 2006–2007);
- Patrons will have their own views and interests, which will be part of how they learn digital literacy (Cornelius, 2004; Floridi, 2002); and, most holistically,
- Providing free access to information is an inherently political act (Knox, 2013).

These considerations can be made more tangible by thinking about teaching digital literacy to a middle school student doing research on civil rights protests. If the first result the student gets in a search is the site of a hate group and the second is a news parody site, a librarian who does not explain the true nature of these sites and how to try to identify similar untrustworthy sources of information may be maintaining neutrality but is certainly not fulfilling his or her role as an educator.

In continuing to hew to this neutral stance, libraries have boxed themselves in as far as the ability to advocate for their own needs and the needs of their communities. By simultaneously declaring themselves central to democracy and above the world of politics that all other public institutions inhabit, libraries have "evolved into a paradox" (Shavit, 1986, p. 3). Political and policy decisions shape what libraries can do, but libraries commonly say they want nothing to do with politics and policy. The result is a self-imposed voicelessness on many important issues with dramatic impacts on libraries, including their ability to articulate and demonstrate their central roles to human rights and social justice (Jaeger & Bertot, 2011; Jaeger, Bertot, & Gorham, 2013; Jaeger, Gorham, Bertot, & Sarin, 2014). If they wish to change perceptions and receive credit—and more importantly support—as institutions of human rights and social justice, libraries must drop the stance of neutrality, step through the threshold, and embrace their profound contributions to their communities. One way that has been suggested to begin to address these needs is through the use of social media, such as Wikipedia, to very publicly catalog, explain, and demonstrate the human rights and social justice contributions of libraries (McCook, 2014).

ARSENALS OF HUMAN RIGHTS AND SOCIAL JUSTICE

Libraries are a central part of the human rights and social justice infrastructure, but they need to better articulate and advocate based on these roles both inside and outside of the library profession to encourage better understanding of and support for libraries' unique and varied contributions to fostering rights and justice. One difficulty is operationalizing, articulating, and demonstrating the contributions that the field is making to human rights and social justice. The other difficulty is adjusting the self-perceptions and expectations to better meet the realities of the myriad rights and justice activities that define librarianship. This search for the best ways to express and claim libraries' part of rights and justice has been a challenge for librarians, who have been far better at engaging in these activities than at explaining their contributions to those outside of libraries.

Advocacy, quite simply, is necessary for survival for publicly supported institutions (Hussey & Velasquez, 2011; Imhoff, 2006; Nelson, 2006). Along with becoming more committed to advocacy, libraries must also reenvision the ways in which to package themselves through advocacy. Unfortunately, the lack of advocacy and marketing training or a culture of lobbying limit the ability and willingness of libraries to market their services, which is increasingly an expectation for public service entities (R. Parker, Kaufman-Scarborough, & Parker, 2007). Regardless of the type of library, articulating the message of being a rights and justice organization and advocating for funding for the library's true contributions to the service community is an essential activity. Public, school, academic, and special libraries may have different funding sources and different funding models, but all need to advocate. Public libraries and school libraries need support in local government and local populations; academic libraries must negotiate for their funding with provosts and university systems; and special libraries may need to advocate to a range of funders, but whether it is within a corporation, a government agency, or another context, they need to advocate for support.

Suggestions have been made for several years now that a stronger focus on libraries as essential educational institutions would serve them well in advocating for funding and other forms of support (Crowley, 2005; Crowley & Ginsberg, 2005). This also extends to the evaluation research libraries conduct to explain what they do—assessments of the social impact of libraries have rarely been a key part of library evaluation studies, but they need to become much more common if a true picture of library contributions is to emerge (Debono, 2002).

When the Internet first became prevalent in libraries, many librarians focused on the technical implications—such as access to electronic resources, digital preservation, and increasing technology availability—with one author proclaiming that the technologies were ushering in a new "Golden Age of Libraries" (Bennett, 2001, p. 256). However, the focus on the technical capacities, rather than the educational activities of libraries, has helped to blur the library and the technology in the minds of many people. This is an unfortunate association, as technology can be found in many places, but digital literacy education and digital inclusion services are very hard to find outside of a library. A closer metaphor was also offered in 2001: "Cornerstones of Liberty" (Kranich, 2001), but even that does not fully capture what libraries now do for their communities.

As the examples and cases described through this book reveal, libraries of all types are truly institutions that fuel rights and justice in their communities. To update a phrase to describe post–World War II libraries, the contemporary library is an arsenal of human rights and social justice. Today, a library cannot simply present materials, it needs to "positively impact library patrons' interest in becoming more critically engaged and foster a greater understanding of the issues raised" by the materials (Cocciolo, 2013, p. 1). Libraries are sustaining equity and inclusion in their communities, educating individual community members, and building stronger communities. To be viewed and supported by others for the contributions they provide, libraries need to begin to advocate in terms of their roles as arsenals of human rights and social justice.

The actual work of all professions changes on a regular basis, so libraries must focus on advocacy, marketing, and self-perceptions that tie into the core reason for their existence, not the specific activities at any given moment (Abbott, 1998). Since the advent of the Internet as a tool for libraries to make new contributions to their communities—and the simultaneous decline of many other institutions that had helped to sustain the public good—the work of the library has matured into ever-greater community contributions. Library professionals are educators and social service providers and community organizers who happen to specialize in information.

Each fall, in the master's course on human rights, social justice, and information offered by the University of Maryland, the students are almost all future librarians. Many of them enter the course already thinking of librarianship as a profession devoted to rights and justice. For these students, the biggest hurdle in the course is finding ways to express the contributions to rights and justice that libraries make in language that clearly articulates those contributions and then using data that demonstrates those contributions. For many of the other future librarians in school, however, they have yet to make this leap, and they still struggle to think of libraries as centers of rights and justice, in large part because our educational programs reflect the field's general failure to consider these issues beyond practice.

Classes on these topics are quite rare in library education programs. A 2010 study found that only 22.2 percent of recent LIS graduates had the option to take a course related to diversity and inclusion in their degree programs, and only 21.3 percent felt they were prepared by their degree to work with diverse populations (Mestre, 2010). Such findings are saddening but not surprising. Across library programs, neither required courses nor the vast majority of regularly offered electives at LIS programs typically focus on any types of issues of diversity and inclusion. The electives that do focus on these issues are rarely offered in most programs (Jaeger, Bertot, & Subramaniam, 2013; Subramaniam & Jaeger, 2010, 2011; Subramaniam, Rodriguez-Mori, Jaeger, & Franklin Hill, 2012). A 2014 survey found 67 percent of respondents noting some course content related to diversity in their LIS program and 54 percent noting some course content related to social equity (Jakowska, Smith, & Buehler, 2014), but it is hard to place overmuch value on these percentages, as the survey did not use sampling and only had fifty-eight respondents from all LIS school employees and graduates.

For the more holistic approaches to these topics as issues of human rights and social justice, only a few institutions, such as the University of Maryland, the University of Illinois, and the University of South Florida offer students the opportunity to take classes devoted to the topics (Jaeger, Cooke, Feltis, Hamiel, Jardine, & Shilton, 2015). Only Maryland offers the opportunity for MLS students to specialize in these areas. Yet, many LIS educators, professionals, and professional organizations acknowledge and are committed to increasing diversity in field (Adkins, Virden, & Yier, 2015; Hastings, 2015).

The failure of LIS education to give more emphasis to these areas means that soon-to-be librarians are not sufficiently prepared for the realities of the profession that they are entering. In a great many institutions, being a librarian means being a combination information expert, educator, and social service provider. This unique combination of skills makes librarians absolutely essential to their communities and very hard to replace. Most teachers are not experts in information and technology, and neither are most social workers. Librarians in public, academic, school, and many special libraries, on the other hand, have to balance and interweave all three of these roles into their average workday (Cathcart, 2008; Westbrook, 2015).

Sadly, this very essence of librarianship—the thing that makes libraries uniquely vital in their ability to serve their communities—is not central to library education. In 1950, library school curriculum across programs tended to focus on administration, collection development, reference, classification, and history (Leigh, 1950). Many of the MLS programs today are distressingly closer to 1950 in what they teach than preparing their students to work in an arsenal of rights and justice. Yet, simply paying attention to current events demonstrates the extent to which the world has changed in terms of information as an issue of rights and justice.

On October 14, 2014, as an example, the front section of the *Washington Post* featured four articles about information being central to limitations of rights and justice in four different nations. In China, the government began to censor books by writers seen as supportive of pro-democracy demonstrators in addition to the already active censorship of online materials related to the protests and the arrests of protest leaders (Wan, 2014). In Russia, the government shut down the oldest human rights organization in the country for documenting abuses committed by the Soviet-era government (Birnbaum, 2014). In Jordan, sharing comments, photos, and videos online about any topic the government disapproves of was classified as an act of terrorism against the state (Booth & Luck, 2014). In the United States, protests in Ferguson, Missouri, continued over the police shooting of an unarmed teenager, as well as in response to police tactics to silence critics and withhold information about the shooting (Lowery & Hernandez, 2014).

Information has become the ultimate rights and justice issue in a world defined by the Internet; to fail to prepare future librarians for this world does a disservice to them, to the libraries in which they will work, and to the communities that these libraries serve. Preliminary studies of the growing education and social work of librarianship reveal that many current librarians feel ill informed about and ill prepared for the human rights and social justice aspects of librarianship (Westbrook, 2015).

Library education is not alone in this neglect; human rights education is significantly lacking internationally (Suarez, 2007). However, as a profession that is centered on equity and inclusion and rights and justice, library education needs to pay more attention to these issues than other professions. When they are prepared to be professionals focused on rights and justice, students in our field are eager to use the skills and ideas from library school to foster change in their communities and promote inclusion. In addition, learning to explain the roles of libraries in the language of human rights and social justice is extremely valuable in describing the contributions and value of libraries to government agencies, funders, policy makers, and other organizations promoting social justice.

Chapter Eight

From Fire, By Fire: Rights and Justice in Policy, Practice, and Advocacy

In nature, animals that live in large groups—whether flocks or herds or schools or packs—tend to be safer in the middle of that group. The group members at the edges are often more vulnerable to predation or to be becoming lost, while those that are more central have the safety of the crowd. Though humans are not stalked by predators in the same manner, the social interactions of people also favor the survivability of those that stay close to the center of norms, values, ethics, and beliefs.

Those at the ideological edges sometimes achieve great success and fame, at least for a time, such as Senator Joe McCarthy riding anticommunist hysteria to national power and prominence for several years before being exposed as a fear-mongering fraud. The majority of long-lasting politicians are typically those that stick to mainstream, popular stances. The same is true for other public figures. Celebrities who engage in political and social controversies and take unpopular stances often do so to the detriment of their careers. "People usually last longer, living in the middle" (McKinney, 2012, p. 224).

In this context, libraries have managed to walk a delicate line for many, many years. They have repeatedly taken progressive actions that challenge the mainstream views of the nation and of their communities in areas such as integration, censorship, inclusion, education, privacy, and a range of other issues of rights and justice discussed in this book. Though some in the profession have long argued that libraries are politically neutral institutions, their actions loudly refute such positions (Jaeger, Gorham, Bertot, & Sarin, 2014; Jaeger, Gorham, Sarin, & Bertot, 2013). Yet, in spite of such activism and challenging of mainstream opinions, libraries remain a mostly beloved social institution. The punishment they face is not ceasing to exist, but in-

115

stead having insufficient support and being marginalized in decision-making processes.

In 1931, Arnold Borden observed that "although next to the public school system and the press the library exercises the greatest educative influence in the state, it rarely appears to be given much weight in deliberations of sociologists and political scientists" (p. 278). This same statement could be made today and would be even more apt. Along with generally being ignored by those that study the ways in which society functions, libraries are cut out of policy-making and political processes. As a result, decisions are made that have enormous consequences for libraries without involving libraries in the process or considering the ramifications for libraries (Jaeger, Gorham, Bertot, & Sarin, 2014).

SEARCHING THROUGH THE DARKNESS

For the past several decades, as was discussed in chapter 2, the political and social discourse in the United States has become dominated by neoliberal economic and neoconservative political ideologies. The neoconservative political ideology is based on the belief that the state should exercise power as moral authority rather than through representative governance, while the neoliberal economic ideology mandates that decisions of governance be based on what is best for markets, meaning that economic, political, and social decisions are all driven by market concerns and organized by the language and rationality of markets. The confluence of these ideologies has been labeled the "American nightmare" (Brown, 2006, p. 690).

This ideological combination is "consistently hostile to the public realm," seeking to replace public goods with "the rule of private interests, coordinated by the markets" (J. Clarke, 2004, pp. 30–31). Through this focus on the private sector, many agencies of the public good found in urban areas—cafes, museums, bookstores, lecture halls, and parks—have dissipated significantly in recent decades (Cohen, 2003; Dean, 2013). A large number of major policy and political ideas that have become mainstream and widely implemented since the beginning of Ronald Reagan's presidency in 1981 are implementations of neoliberal economic beliefs, such as:

- The deregulation of the private sector is based on strengthening the ability of corporations at the expense of individuals, assuming that the market will find ways to protect individuals through options.
- The widespread use of school choice, charter schools, and school vouchers stems from the neoliberal belief that the market will provide better options than government, even if many of the new educational options are not particularly successful at providing an education.

- State governments have been disbanding or disempowering unions that represent public employees to reduce costs and shrink the size and influence of government.
- Public schools are being underwritten by corporate sponsorships and vending machine contracts.
- The National Performance Review studies were conducted by President Bill Clinton's administration to focus on efficiency, productivity, and profitability rather than good governance or the public good.
- President George W. Bush proposed (ultimately unsuccessfully) to change Social Security to individual retirement accounts, under which citizens would have been left to fend for themselves in the market.

The impacts of these policies have significantly reshaped the size and capacity of government. Based on recent Bureau of Labor Statistics (BLS) data, 680,000 public sector jobs in the United States were lost between June 2009 and August 2012, or roughly 3 percent of the local, state, and federal government jobs that existed before the prolonged economic downturn began (BLS, 2012). In 2011 alone, state and local governments cut nearly 250,000 jobs (Governing, 2014).

Prior to the widespread embrace of the neoliberal economic ideology by politicians, sociologists and historians had made clear that degrading the public sphere in favor of the private sphere serves to undermine the value of both the public and private spheres as elements to support a functional society (Sennett, 1974). In supporting the public good, governments can provide services, distributions, and stabilization of the market, none of which the market itself can provide as effectively, or at all in many cases, as it focuses on monetizing discrete services to individuals provided by different companies (Ver Eecke, 1998, 1999). Yet, the neoliberal economic ideology has driven the reductions in funding that have harmed many public institutions, including libraries.

The implementation of the neoconservative political ideology has also been very hard on the public sector, particularly institutions of education. Neoconservatism belittles educational institutions, like schools and libraries, as serving to erode the values of the supposed majority. The values of neoconservatism are often evidenced through language celebrating the "traditional" family unit and "pro-family" perspectives that are rooted in opposition to rights for many disadvantaged populations through politics and policy (Burnham, 2010; Gaffney, 2013). Neoconservatism is designed to appeal to the upper and middle classes, creating a narrative that they, as the wealthy, hegemonic majority, are besieged by minority groups and the disadvantaged who are trying to change their way of life. The neoconservative political ideology has succeeded in getting large segments of the middle and upper classes to believe that they need protection from the government, rather than focusing on the reality of receiving the considerable benefits of the government that accrue to the advantaged populations (Burnham, 2010).

As state steerage of the economy is central to the neoconservative approach, its economic dimensions have simply become the same as the neoliberal economic ideology. Under the combination of these two ideologies, economic discourse now "prescribes the form that 'problems' have to be given before they can be acted upon, the kinds of 'choices' that exist, and the meaning of 'rationality'" and frames the discussion and choices in "virtually every sphere of public activity, from health care, social welfare, and education to weapons systems, environmental protection, and scientific research" (Wolin, 1981, pp. 26–28). This approach to policy encourages divisions and promotes inequalities in availability and funding of public services (Wolin, 1993).

Since the combination of these ideologies swept into the political mainstream, the result has been radical change through reductions in tax rates, spending cuts for public services, deregulation, and erosions of social support for the public good. In a public discourse in which every public good can be questioned and required to demonstrate a tangible value, economic terminology began to dominate public discourse. Corporations are also much more likely than individuals to garner political support and funding for the infrastructure on which they depend. "What is missing is investment in such things as public libraries, parks, city streets and sidewalks, urban mass transit" (Galbraith, 1998, p. 207).

At all levels of society, political problems have been transformed into individual problems with market solutions (Brown, 2006). Libraries, while they contribute enormously to their communities, are not likely to turn a profit for a company or for a government. As a result, libraries now stand as the "symbol of the impoverishment of the public domain" (Newman, 2007, p. 905). Ultimately, under the twined ideologies of neoliberalism and neoconservatism, libraries are injured in three interrelated ways: they are distrusted as educational institutions, they are not given a voice in policy and political decisions that impact them, and they are defunded as entities that do not produce a profit (Jaeger, Gorham, Bertot, & Sarin, 2014). Libraries have not been destroyed for being outside of the middle, but they certainly are feeling the effects of straying from places of safety.

THE BREAKS IN THE SKY

At the tail end of the last millennium, Kofi Annan, the seventh secretary general of the UN, stated: "People lack many things: jobs, shelter, food, health care, and drinkable water. Today, being cut off from basic telecommunications services is a hardship almost as acute as these other deprivations, and may indeed reduce the chances of finding remedies to them" (1999). Fifteen years later, as this book has argued in detail, the observation still holds true. In the intervening years, the ability to access, use, and understand ICTs has become far more important to education, employment, social inclusion, civic engagement, and much else that could have been imagined in 1999. Now, guarantees of human rights and social justice are dependent on information, and the ability to use information is its own issue of rights and justice.

Not surprisingly, in an environment shaped by neoliberal and neoconservative ideologies, "the whole idea of human rights has lost some of its romantic appeal and moral authority" (Moyn, 2012, n.p.). Stances supporting human rights and social justice often take a long time to have visible impacts (De Mesquita et al., 2005), which makes them even harder to get support for in a political climate focused on businesslike results from governing. Libraries—as the public institutions that protect rights and promote justice through information, inclusion, access, education, and services—are making an inherently brave stand in a political climate that prioritizes private action and corporate entities. But this stand is also extremely necessary, as no other institutions are left to meet these vital individual and community needs.

In an earlier book (Jaeger, Gorham, Bertot, & Sarin, 2014), we suggested that libraries need to see themselves—and encourage others to see them—as a *community good*. The idea behind this term is to promote the view of libraries as being more than just a part of the *public good*, as was discussed earlier in this book. Unlike other public goods, the more that a library is supported, the more value to the community it generates and the more members of the community that it helps. Much of what makes a library a community good is tied to the activities that it engages in to protect human rights and promote social justice for individuals and entire communities.

The more plentiful and stable library funding and public support are, the more people the library can help. By providing a greater number of services, resources, and materials and increasing its involvement in community partnerships, a library can increase the impact that it has on its community. The scope of the good generated by the library grows with the amount of support given to the library. Due to their resources and the skills of staff members, libraries can become centers for literacy and inclusion, education, civic engagement, social services, emergency response and recovery, e-government, job training, and innumerable other contributions to the health of the community and its members, so long as they are provided sufficient support.

All of the contributions to human rights and social justice discussed in this book grow with the support provided to libraries. The library is a good that can adapt and expand the amount of good it provides to the community—and the depth of the support it can provide to human rights and social justice—through proportional increases in funding. Many different elements make the library a community good, but the human rights and social justice roles encapsulate the concept of the community good better than any other contributions that libraries make to their patrons and their communities.

However, just as libraries can do more to promote human rights and social justice with greater resources, they inevitably are able to do less when their funding is reduced or other forms of support are weakened. Since 2009, when the Great Recession began, most libraries have experienced decreased budgets and increased usage year after year (Jaeger, Gorham, Bertot, & Sarin, 2014). As an example, in the most recent annual library budget survey published by *Library Journal*, overall state funding for libraries fell 8.3 percent, with 44 percent of respondents observing a decrease in state funding (Schwartz, 2013). When the resources decline, libraries often make exceptional efforts to continue to provide uninterrupted services, but continual declines cannot help but to cut into the ability of libraries to support human rights and social justice.

When the position of libraries as institutions of human rights and social justice is weakened by insufficient resources, the impacts extend beyond what the library does. The status of human rights and social justice in the community is weakened overall, as libraries are less able to create partnerships with other community organizations to meet rights and justice needs. There are also fewer library materials and services available for use by other groups to promote their own activities to promote human rights and social justice in the community. Libraries may uniquely expose themselves as public institutions that do not stay at the middle of the pack, but many other individual, groups, and organizations suffer when libraries suffer.

The situation is not all storm clouds and darkness; not all falls the shadow. There are breaks in the sky as well. Progressive, community-oriented issues seem to be getting greater support than they have received in recent years, none more notable than the large number of states that have implemented marriage equality laws in the past two years. Movements emphasizing community gardens to urban renewal indicate that at least a portion of the population is paying greater attention to the health of the community (Dudley, 2013). Additionally, the oldest members of the millennial generation (young adults aged eighteen to thirty-three) are generally more supportive than older Americans of a larger government that provides more services (Pew Research Center, 2014). Libraries have the opportunity to link to these community-minded interests, clearly articulating the centrality of their roles in ensuring human rights and social justice in their communities. They just have to learn to tell the story.

FROM FIRE, BY FIRE

We have used the phrase "becoming what they already are" in this book to demonstrate the need for the members of the library profession to embrace what they already are and what libraries already do as institutions of human rights and social justice and as the backbone of the community good. A key part of thinking of themselves in these terms is telling others of their activities and roles in the language of human rights, social justice, and the community good. "We do not sing our praises loudly enough. We do not tell our stories compellingly enough. We do not take credit for our achievements, and we certainly do not assert our position as the very public heart and soul of the information age" (Kent, 1996, p. 212). Librarians need to communicate, research, market, and advocate for themselves in terms of promoting human rights and social justice and supporting the community good.

Many resources provide detailed descriptions of how libraries can market what they do, advocate for more support, and communicate their message to encourage public support and support in policy-making, political, and funding processes. Many are very good resources that offer useful ideas and approaches. In the two companion books to this one, we offer extensive plans for advocacy, marketing, and policy and political engagement that members of the library profession can use in their efforts to receive something closer to the support that they need to serve their communities in all of the ways in which they have the ability to help (Jaeger, Gorham, Bertot, & Sarin, 2014; Thompson, Jaeger, Taylor, Subramaniam, & Bertot, 2014).

Rather than reiterating the points about the importance of and approaches to advocacy, communication, outreach, and marketing made in our previous texts and by many other publications, this book will close by mapping the necessity of implementing these approaches effectively around the human rights and social justice roles of libraries when communicating with the members of the public, other government agencies, policy makers, funders, and politicians. The key themes of the book are the main messages that libraries need to begin to convey through advocacy, communication, outreach, and marketing in order to receive sufficient support in financial, political, and policy realms so as to render them capable of meeting the community needs they are already trying to address. To encapsulate:

• Libraries ensure information access, literacy, and digital inclusion. All of these are necessary for equity and social inclusion. They are also the foundations of all human rights, both being rights in themselves and underlying other rights.
• For human rights to be effectively implemented, they depend on systems of social justice; for systems of social justice to be relevant, they need to be built upon a framework of recognized human rights. Libraries support

both rights and justice, and in many contexts directly ensure rights and justice.

- Libraries are community anchors that promote social justice and human rights through a wide range of their activities, including education and literacy, social inclusion, social services, community outreach, partnerships with other community groups, and provision of access to printed materials, electronic materials, and the online environment.
- While the contributions may vary by type of library, all libraries—public, school, academic, and others—make myriad, clear contributions to human rights and social justice.
- No other institutions are capable of serving as many rights and justice roles as libraries. As a community good, libraries can meet as many individual and community needs as the financial, political, and other support will allow.
- Through partnerships with and support of other community organizations and local government agencies, libraries accomplish many rights and justice goals in conjunction with other organizations.
- Even though they are already filling these amazing human rights and social justice roles—ensuring access, inclusion, and equity for individuals and entire communities—the members of the library profession do not speak of libraries as or frame library activities as institutions of rights and justice.
- If the members of the library profession were to embrace the reality of the roles that they are already playing, it would provide many new opportunities to connect their activities to members of the public, to demonstrate their value to policy makers, politicians, and funders, and to articulate the reasons that libraries remain vital and necessary institutions in the time of smartphones and social media.

These messages can be used to counteract misperceptions about libraries and argue for greater funding and other types of support. But to be effective, these arguments must be made. The ideas presented in this book are meant to help start a much bigger dialogue on these issues and their ramifications for the future of the profession, as such discussions are important to a great many people in society.

Libraries and library professionals are not the only ones whose well-being depends on the library profession better expressing and advocating around the human rights and social justice activities. Many individuals, many populations, and many organizations in a community—that is, a large segment of each community—depend on the human rights and social justice roles that libraries fulfill. Without libraries, most of these rights and justice needs would go unmet. Libraries are filling these roles for the benefit of their communities, and so they also need to articulate and advocate around these roles for the benefit of the communities. Continued success as institutions of rights and justice depends on embracing and articulating these roles.

Librarians are information-enabled educators, social service providers, and community builders. They are service-oriented community leaders (Bertot & Sarin, 2015); they are "learning alchemists" (Taylor, Surbamaniam, & Waugh, 2015, p. 38). Libraries enable, include, empower, and educate in ways that no other community institution can. These qualities of libraries and librarians are what make our profession and our institutions vital to our patrons and our communities, as well as to the promotion of human rights and social justice both in our communities and in society as a whole.

As arsenals of human rights and social justice, libraries are now serving their communities in a wide range of ways that could not have been imagined even twenty years ago. In spite of the seeming omnipresence of mobile technologies and the interconnectedness of social media, libraries are the hope for human rights and social justice in most communities. The years of neoconservative political and neoliberal economic ideologies—particularly the years of the Great Recession—have been a trial by fire for libraries in many ways. Such fire can either serve to destroy or can hone to a finer, stronger state.

The events faced by libraries over recent years have helped libraries to mature into centers of human rights and social justice for their communities, a role in which they are currently thriving in spite of the seemingly limitless political, policy, and financial challenges. For libraries the struggle is not doing well in these areas, it is finding the support to continue to do more and better moving forward. Embracing the role of arsenals of human rights and social justice—becoming what they already are—is the path by which libraries can frame their inclusion, equity, literacy, access, education, and social service activities in ways that can best encourage the support they need to continue to promote rights and justice in their communities.

References

Abbott, A. (1998). Professionalism and the future of librarianship. *Library Trends, 46*, 430–443.

Abel, J. (2013). Ineffective assistance of the library: The failings and the future of prison law libraries. *Georgetown Law Journal, 101*, 1171–1216.

Acosta, L. M., & Cherry, A. M. (2007). Reference services in courts and governmental settings. *Legal Reference Services Quarterly, 26*(1–2), 113–134.

Adkins, D., Virden, C., & Yier, C. (2015). Learning about diversity: The roles of LIS education, LIS associations, and lived experience. *Library Quarterly, 85*, 139–148.

Albitz, B. (2005). Dude, where are my civil rights? *Journal of Academic Librarianship, 31*(3), 284–286.

Alfino, M., & Pierce, L. (2001). *Information ethics for librarians.* Jefferson, NC: McFarland.

Alfino, M., & Pierce, L. (2001). The social nature of information. *Library Trends, 49*, 471–485.

American Association of School Librarians (AASL). (2009). *Empowering learners: Guidelines for school library media programs.* Chicago: American Library Association.

American Library Association (ALA). (n.d.) *Creating family literacy focus initiatives.* Available: http://www.ala.org/advocacy/literacy/earlyliteracy/famlitfocus

American Library Association (ALA). (1996). *Library bill of rights.* Available: http://www.ala.org/advocacy/intfreedom/librarybill

American Library Association (ALA). (2001). *Recommendation on privatization of publicly funded libraries.* Available: http://www.ala.org

American Library Association. (2003). *Resolution on the USA PATRIOT Act and related measures that infringe on the rights of library users.* Available: http://www.ala.org

American Library Association (ALA). (2004a). *Core values of librarianship.* Available: http://www.ala.org/advocacy/intfreedom/statementspols/corevalues

American Library Association (ALA). (2004b). *The Freedom to Read Statement.* Available: http://www.ala.org/advocacy/intfreedom/statementspols/freedomreadstatement

American Library Association. (2007). *Resolution on the use and abuse of National Security Letters.* Available: http://www.ala.org

American Library Association (ALA). (2010a). *Keys to engaging older adults @ your library.* Office for Literacy and Outreach Services. Available: http://www.ala.org/offices/sites/ala.org.offices/files/content/olos/toolkits/olderadults/oat.sequential.pdf

American Library Association (ALA). (2010b). *Libraries Connect Communities: Public Library Funding & Technology Access Study 2009–2010.* Chicago: American Library Association. Available: http://www.ala.org/plinternetfunding/

American Library Association (ALA). (2011). *Keeping public libraries public: A checklist for communities considering privatization of public libraries.* Available: http://www.ala.org

American Library Association (ALA). (2012a). *ALA policy manual.* Available: http://www.ala.org

American Library Association (ALA). (2012b). *Extending our reach: Reducing homelessness through library engagement.* Office for Literacy and Outreach Services. Available: http://www.ala.org/offices/sites/ala.org.offices/files/content/olos/toolkits/poorhomeless_FINAL.pdf

American Library Association (ALA). (2013a). *Declaration for the right to libraries.* Available: http://www.ala.org

American Library Association (ALA). (2013b). *Día! Diversity in action.* Available: http://dia.ala.org/

American Library Association (ALA). (2013c). The state of America's libraries—2013. *American Libraries.* Available: http://www.ala.org/news/state-americas-libraries-report-2013

American Library Association (ALA). (2014a). *ALA troubled by court's net neutrality decision.* Available: http://www.ala.org

American Library Association (ALA). (2014b). *Core values, ethics, and core competencies. Policy Manual, Section B.1.* Available: http://www.ala.org

American Library Association (ALA). (2014c). *Net neutrality: Advocacy, legislation & issues.* Available: http://www.ala.org

Annan, K. (1999). Comments at Telecomm 99 + Interactive 99. Available: www.itu.int/itunews/issue/1999/09/telec99.html

Arrigo, P. A. (2004). The reinvention of the FDLP: A paradigm shift from product provider to service provider. *Journal of Government Information, 30*(5), 684–709.

Association of College and Research Libraries (ACRL). (2000). *Information literacy competency standards for higher education.* Chicago: American Library Association.

Audunson, R., Essmat, S., & Aabo, S. (2011). Public libraries: A meeting place for immigrant women? *Library & Information Science Research, 33*, 220–227.

Augst, T. (2001). Introduction: Libraries and agencies of culture. In T. Augst & W. Wiegand (Eds.), *Libraries as agencies of culture* (pp. 5–22). Madison: University of Wisconsin Press.

Augst, T. (2007). Faith in reading: Public libraries, liberalism, and the civil religion. In T. Augst & K. Carpenter (Eds.), *Institutions of reading: The social life of libraries in the United States* (pp. 148–183). Amherst: University of Massachusetts Press.

Auld, H. S. (2004). Patrons, customers, users, clients. *Public Libraries, 43*(2), 81–87.

Baldwin, R. W. (1966). *Social justice.* Oxford: Pergamon.

Banisar, D. (2006). The right to information in the information age. In R. F. Jorgensen (Ed.), *Human rights in the global information society* (pp. 73–90). Cambridge, MA: MIT Press.

Barack, L. (2014, July 9). Bridging the gap: Making libraries more accessible for a diverse autistic population. *School Library Journal.* Available: http://www.slj.com/2014/07/programs/bridging-the-gap-making-libraries-more-accessible-for-a-diverse-autistic-population/#

Barber, B. R. (1997). The new telecommunications technology: Endless frontier or the end of democracy? *Constellations, 4*, 208–228.

Barry, B. (1989). *Theories of justice.* Berkeley: University of California Press.

Baschuk, B. (2014, July 10). FCC chairman's E-Rate proposal dogged by funding controversies. *Bloomberg BNA.* Available: http://www.bna.com/fcc-chairmans-erate-n17179892064/

Batch, K. R. (2014). *Fencing out knowledge: Impacts of the Children's Internet Protection Act 10 years later.* Washington, DC: American Library Association Office of Information Technology Policy.

Baumgartner, F. R., Berry, J. M., Hojnacki, M., Leech, B. L., & Kimball, D. C. (2009). *Lobbying and policy change: Who wins, who loses, and why.* Chicago: University of Chicago Press.

Becker, S., Crandall, M. D., Fisher, K. E., Kinney, B., Landry, C., & Rocha, A. (2010). *Opportunity for all: How the American public benefits from Internet access at U.S. libraries.* Washington, DC: Institute for Museum and Library Services. Available: http://impact.ischool.washington.edu/documents/OPP4ALL_FinalReport.pdf

Behr, T. C. (2003). *Luigi Taparelli on the dignity of man*. Rome: Congresso Tomista Internazionale.

Bell, C. J. (2006). Libraries and human rights education. *Catholic Library World, 77*(2), 112–119.

Bennett, S. (2001). The golden age of libraries. *Journal of Academic Librarianship, 27*, 256–259.

Berenson, S. K. (2001). A family law residency program? A modest proposal in response to the burdens created by self-represented litigants in family court. *Rutgers Law Journal, 33*(1), 105–164.

Berlin, I. (1979). *Four essays on liberty*. Oxford: Oxford University Press.

Berman, S. (1998, March). On my mind—Libraries, class, and the poor people's policy. *American Libraries, 29*, 38.

Berninghausen, D. K. (1948a). Book-banning and witch hunts. *American Library Association Bulletin, 42*(5), 204.

Berninghausen, D. K. (1948b). Current attacks on books. *American Library Association Bulletin, 42*(5), 58.

Berninghausen, D. K. (1953). The history of the ALA Intellectual Freedom Committee. *Wilson Library Bulletin, 27*(10), 813–817.

Berry, J. N., & Rawlinson, N. (1991). No time for neutrality. *Library Journal*. Available: http://www.libraryjournal.com

Bertot, J. C. (2003). The multiple dimensions of the digital divide: More than technology "haves" and "have-nots." *Government Information Quarterly, 20*, 185–191.

Bertot, J. C. (2009). Public access technologies in public libraries: Impacts and implications. *Information Technology & Libraries, 28*(2), 84–95.

Bertot, J. C. (2014). Closing one chapter, opening another: Moving *Library Quarterly* forward. *Library Quarterly, 84*(4), 489–490.

Bertot, J. C., Gorham, U., Jaeger, P. T., & Taylor, N. G. (2012). Public libraries and the Internet 2012: Key findings, recent trends, and future challenges. *Public Library Quarterly, 31*, 303–325.

Bertot, J. C., & Jaeger, P. T. (2012). Implementing and managing public library networks, connectivity, and partnerships to promote e-government access and education. In S. Aikins (Ed.), *Managing e-government projects: Concepts, issues, and best practices* (pp. 183–199). Hershey, PA: IGI Global.

Bertot, J. C., Jaeger, P. T., & Greene, N. N. (2013). Transformative e-government and public service: Public libraries in times of economic hardship. In V. Weerakkody & C. G. Reddick (Eds.), *Public sector transformation through e-government: Experiences from Europe and North America* (pp. 35–46). New York: Routledge.

Bertot, J. C., Jaeger, P. T., Lee, J., Dubbels, K., McDermott, A., & Real, B. M. (2014). *2013 Digital Inclusion survey: Survey findings and results*. College Park, MD: Information Policy and Access Center.

Bertot, J. C., Jaeger, P. T., McClure, C. R., Wright, C. B., & Jensen, E. (2009). Public libraries and the Internet 2008–2009: Issues, implications, and challenges. *First Monday, 14*(11). Available: http://firstmonday.org/ojs/fm/article/view/2700/2351

Bertot, J. C., Jaeger, P. T., & Sarin, L. C. (2012). *Forbes* folly: The lessons of being labeled the worst master's degree. *American Libraries, 43*(9–10), 30–33.

Bertot, J. C., Jaeger, P. T., Shuler, J. A., Simmons, S. N., & Grimes, J. M. (2009). Reconciling government documents and e-government: Government information in policy, librarianship, and education. *Government Information Quarterly, 26*, 433–436.

Bertot, J. C., & McClure, C. R. (1999). Public library Internet connectivity: Status and policy implications. *Library & Information Science Research, 21*, 281–298.

Bertot, J. C., McDermott, A., Lincoln, R., Real, B., & Peterson, K. (2012). *2011–2012 Public library funding and technology access survey: Survey findings and results*. College Park, MD: Information Policy and Access Center. Available: http://plinternetsurvey.org/sites/default/files/publications/2012_plftas.pdf

Bertot, J. C., & Sarin, L. (2015). The future of MLS: Rethinking library education. *American Libraries, 46*(3/4), 40–42.

Birkland, T. A. (2001). *Introduction to the policy process*. Armonk, NY: Sharpe.

Birnbaum, M. (2014, October 14). Russia moves to disband chronicler of Soviet-era persecutions. *Washington Post*, p. A9.

Blanke, H. T. (1989). Librarianship and political values: Neutrality or commitment? *Library Journal, 114*(7), 39–43.

Blau, J., & Moncada, A. (2006). *Human Rights and the U.S. Constitution*. Lanham, MD: Rowman & Littlefield.

Blue, E. V., & Pace, D. (2011). UD and UDL: Paving the way toward inclusion and independence in the school library. *Knowledge Quest, 39*(3), 49–55.

Blumenstein, L. (2009, July 22). In Gainesville, FL, "The Library Partnership" merges branch, social services. *Library Journal*. Available: http://www.libraryjournal.com/

Booth, W., & Luck, T. (2014, October 14). New anti-terror law cracks down on social media activity. *Washington Post*, p. A10.

Borden, A. K. (1931). The sociological beginnings of the library movement. *Library Quarterly, 1*, 278–282.

Borko, H. (1968). Information science: What is it? *American Documentation, 19*(1), 3–5.

Bossaller, J. S. (in press). Access to affordable care through public libraries. *Library Quarterly*.

Boulding, K. E. (1962). Social justice in social dynamics. In R. B. Brandt (Ed.), *Social justice* (pp. 73–92). Englewood Cliffs, NJ: Prentice Hall.

Brandt, R. B. (1962). Preface. In R. B. Brandt (Ed.), *Social justice* (pp. v–vi). Englewood Cliffs, NJ: Prentice Hall.

Branscomb, L. M. (1979). Information: The ultimate frontier. *Science, 203*(4376), 143–147.

Brimhall-Vargas, M. (2015). Where the rubber meets the road: The role of libraries and librarians in bringing equitable access to marginalized communities. *Library Quarterly, 85*, 193–199.

Brito, J., & Dooling, B. (2006, March 25). Who's your daddy? *Wall Street Journal*, p. A9.

Britz, J., Hoffman, A., Ponelis, S., Zimmer, M., & Lor, P. (2013). On considering the application of Amartya Sen's capability approach to an information-based rights framework. *Information Development, 29*(2), 106–113.

Broadband Commission for Digital Development. (n.d.). *Overview*. Available: http://www.broadbandcommission.org/about/overview.aspx

Brophy, P., & Halpin, E. F. (1999). Through the net to freedom: Information, the Internet, and human rights. *Journal of Information Science, 25*, 351–354.

Brown, W. (2006). American nightmare: Neoliberalism, neoconservatism, and de-democratization. *Political Theory, 34*, 690–714.

Buckley, F. J. (1987). Knowledge–access issues. *Information Society, 5*(1), 45–50.

Budd, J. M. (1997, July). A critique of customer and commodity. *College & Research Libraries*, pp. 309–320.

Budd, J. M. (2006). Politics and public library collections. *Progressive Librarian, 28*, 78–86.

Burchardt, T., & Craig, G. (2008). Introduction. In G. Craig, T. Burchardt, & D. Gordon (Eds.), *Social justice and public policy: Seeking fairness in diverse societies* (pp. 11–15). Bristol, UK: Policy Press.

Bureau of Justice Statistics (2013). *Total U.S. correctional population declined in 2012 for fourth straight year*. Available: http://www.bjs.gov/content/pub/press/cpus12pr.cfm

Bureau of Labor Statistics. (2012). *Occupational outlook handbook: Librarians*. Available: http://www.bls.gov/ooh/education-training-and-library/librarians.htm

Burke, S. K. (2008). Use of public libraries by immigrants. *Reference & User Services Quarterly, 48*, 164–174.

Burnett, G., Besant, M., & Chatman, E. A. (2001). Small worlds: Normative behavior in virtual communities and feminist bookselling. *Journal of the American Society for Information Science and Technology, 52*, 536–547.

Burnett, G., & Jaeger, P. T. (2012). Information worlds: Social context and information behavior. In A. Spink & J. Heinstrom (Eds.), *New research in information behaviour* (pp. 161–180). London: Emerald.

Burnett, G., Jaeger, P. T., & Thompson, K. M. (2008). Normative behavior and information: The social aspects of information access. *Library & Information Science Research, 30*(1), 56–66.

Burnham, W. D. (2010). *Democracy in peril: The American turnout problem and the path to plutocracy.* New York: Roosevelt Institute.

Burton, J. (2009). Theory and politics in public librarianship. *Progressive Librarian, 32,* 21–28.

Buschman, J. E. (2003). *Dismantling the public sphere: Situating and sustaining librarianship in the age of the new public philosophy.* Westport, CT: Libraries Unlimited.

Buschman, J. E. (2005). Libraries and the decline of public purposes. *Public Library Quarterly, 24*(1), 1–12.

Buschman, J. E. (2012). *Libraries, classrooms, and the interests of democracy: Marking the limits of neoliberalism.* Lanham, MD: Scarecrow.

Buschman, J. E., Rosenzweig, M., & Harger, E. (1994). The clear imperative for involvement: Librarians must address social issues. *American Libraries, 25*(6), 575–576.

Butler, R. P. (2003). Copyright law and organizing the Internet. *Library Trends, 52,* 307–317.

Byrne, A. (2003). Necromancy or life support? Libraries, democracy and the concerned intellectual. *Library Management, 24,* 116–125.

Caidi, N., & Allard, D. (2005). Social inclusion of newcomers to Canada: An information problem? *Library & Information Science Research, 27,* 302–324.

Calhoun, C. (2007). *Nations matter: Culture, history and the cosmopolitan dream.* London: Routledge.

Carlson, S. (2005). Whose work is it, anyway? *Chronicle of Higher Education, 51*(47), A33–A35.

Caswell, M. (2014). Defining human rights archives: Introduction to the special double issue on archives and human rights. *Archival Science, 14,* 207–213.

Chanen, J. S. (1998). Banned in the bighouse. *ABA Journal, 86,* 26.

Cathcart, R. (2008). Librarian or social worker: Time to look at blurring the line? *Reference Librarian, 49*(1), 87–91.

Chatman, E. A. (1987). Opinion leadership, poverty, and information sharing. *RQ, 26,* 341–353.

Chatman, E. A. (1990). Alienation theory: Application of a conceptual framework to a study of information among janitors. *RQ, 29,* 355–368.

Chatman, E. A. (1991). Channels to a larger world: Older women staying in contact with the great society. *Library & Information Science Research, 13,* 281–300.

Chatman, E. A. (1996). The impoverished life-world of outsiders. *Journal of the American Society for Information Science, 47,* 193–206.

Chatman, E. A. (1999). A theory of life in the round. *Journal of the American Society for Information Science, 50,* 207–217.

Chatman, E. A. (2000). Framing social life in theory and research. *New Review of Information Behaviour Research, 1,* 3–17.

Chatters, C. H. (1957). The outlook for support for public agencies with particular reference to libraries. *Library Quarterly, 27,* 249–254.

Childers, T., & Post, J. (1975). *The information poor in America.* Metuchen, NJ: Scarecrow.

Chu, C. M. (1999). Literacy practices of linguistic minorities: Sociolinguistic issues and implications for literacy services. *Library Quarterly, 69,* 339–359.

Clarke, J. (2004). Dissolving the public realm? The logics and limits of neo-liberalism. *Journal of Social Policy, 33,* 27–48.

Clarke, L. (2014, May 15). Game on (redux) for network neutrality. *ALA District Dispatch.* Available: http://www.districtdispatch.org/2014/05/game-on-redux-network-neutrality

Cocciolo, A. (2013). Public libraries and PBS partnering to enhance civic engagement: A study of a nationwide initiative. *Public Library Quarterly, 32,* 1–20.

Cohen, L. (2003). *A consumer's republic: The politics of mass consumption in postwar America.* New York: Knopf.

Coleman, J. S. (1972). The children have outgrown the schools. *Psychology Today, 5,* 72–75, 82.

Collins, L. N., Howard, F., & Miraflor, A. (2009). Addressing the needs of the homeless: A San José Library partnership approach. *Reference Librarian, 50*(1), 109–116.

Companie, B. M. (1986). Information gaps: Myth or reality? *Telecommunications Policy, 10*(3), 5–12.

Cook, K. J. (2008). *Freedom Libraries in the 1964 Mississippi Freedom Summer Project: A history.* Tuscaloosa: University of Alabama.

Cornelius, I. (2004). Information and its philosophy. *Library Trends, 52,* 377–386.

Cox, R. J. (2011). *The demise of the library school: Personal reflections on professional education in the modern corporate university.* Duluth, MN: Library Juice.

Cramme, O., & Diamond, P. (2009). Rethinking social justice in the global age. In O. Cramme & P. Diamond (Eds.), *Social justice in the global age* (pp. 3–20). Cambridge, UK: Polity.

Cresswell, S. (1996). The last days of Jim Crow in Southern libraries. *Libraries & Culture, 31,* 557–573.

Cronin, B. (2002). What a library is not. *Library Journal, 127*(6), 46.

Crowley, B. (2005). Save professionalism. *Library Journal, 130*(4), 46–48.

Crowley, B., & Ginsberg, D. (2005). Professional values: Priceless. *American Libraries, 36*(1), 52–55.

Cuban, S. (2007). *Serving new immigrant communities in the library.* Westport, CT: Greenwood.

Culnan, M. J. (1983). Environmental scanning: The effects of task complexity and source accessibility on information gathering behavior. *Decision Sciences, 14*(2), 194–206.

Culnan, M. J. (1984). The dimensions of accessibility to online information: Implications for implanting office information systems. *ACM Transactions on Office Information Systems, 2*(2), 141–150.

Culnan, M. J. (1985). The dimensions of perceived accessibility to information: Implications for the delivery of information systems and services. *Journal of the American Society for Information Science, 36*(5), 302–308.

Curry, C., & Grimes, M. (2014). Ferguson library becomes refuge for adults and children amid strife. *ABC News.* Available: http://abcnews.go.com/US/ferguson-library-refuge-adults-children-amid-strife/story?id=25050930

Dana, J. C. (1999). *The new museum: Selected writings by John Cotton Dana.* Ed. by W. A. Peniston. Newark, NJ: Newark Museum Association.

Davies, D. W. (1974). *Public libraries as culture and social centers: The origin of the concept.* Metuchen, NJ: Scarecrow.

Davis, D. M. (2009). Challenges to sustaining library technology. *Public Libraries, 48*(4), 12–17.

Davis, D. M. (2011). Public library funding: An overview and discussion. In J. C. Bertot, P. T. Jaeger, & C. R. McClure (Eds.), *Public libraries and the Internet: Roles, perspectives, and implications* (pp. 193–214). Westport, CT: Libraries Unlimited.

Davlantes, A. (2010, June 28). Are libraries necessary, or a waste of tax money? *Fox News Chicago.*

Dean, J. (2013). Society doesn't exist. *First Monday, 18*(3–4). Available: http://firstmonday.org/ojs/fm/article/view/4616/3419

Debono, B. (2002). Assessing the social impact of public libraries: What the literature is saying. *Australasian Public Libraries and Information Services, 15*(2), 80–95.

De Cindio, F., Gentile, O., Grew, P., & Redolfi, D. (2003). Community networks: Rules of behavior and social structure. *Information Society, 19,* 395–406.

De Mesquita, B. B., Downs, G. W., & Smith, A., & Cherif, M. F. (2005). Thinking inside the box: A closer look at democracy and human rights. *International Studies Quarterly, 49,* 439–457.

Department of Agriculture. (2011). *About the recovery act BIP.* Available: http://www.rurdev.usda.gov/utp_bip.html

Dervin, B. L., & Greenberg, B. S. (1972). The communication environment of the urban poor. *CUP Report No. 15.* East Lansing: Michigan State University Department of Communication.

Dewey, M. (1876). The profession. *American Library Journal, 1,* 5–6.

Dhillon, J. S. (1980). *Information consumption by low income families to reduce rural poverty in Florida.* Tallahassee, FL: Community Development and Research Program, Florida Agricultural and Mechanical University.

DigitalLiteracy.gov. (n.d.). About us. Available: http://www.digitalliteracy.gov/about

Digital Literacy Task Force. (2013). Digital literacy, libraries, and public policy. *American Library Association's Office for Information Technology Policy.* Available: http://www.districtdispatch.org/wp-content/uploads/2013/01/2012_OITP_digilitreport_1_22_13.pdf

Dilevko, J. (2009). *The politics of professionalism: A retro-progressive proposal for librarianship.* Duluth, MN: Library Juice.

Dillon, A., & Norris, A. (2005). Crying wolf: An examination and reconsideration of the perception of crisis in LIS education. *Journal of Education for Library and Information Science, 280*–298.

District of Columbia Public Library. (n.d.) *Adaptive services.* Available: http://dclibrary.org/services/lbph#ATP

District of Columbia Public Library. (2013). *Accessibility hackathon 2.* Available: http://dclibrary.org/node/32540.

Ditzion, S. H. (1947). *Arsenals of a democratic culture.* Chicago: American Library Association.

Dobransky, K., & Hargittai, E. (2006). The disability divide in Internet access and use. *Information Communication & Society, 9,* 313–334.

Doe v. Gonzalez, 386 F. Supp. 2d 66 (2005).

Doyle, C. (2005). *Libraries and the USA PATRIOT Act.* Washington, DC: Congressional Research Service.

Drake, W. J., & Jorgensen, R. F. (2006). Introduction. In R. F. Jorgensen (Ed.), *Human rights in the global information society* (pp. 1–50). Cambridge, MA: MIT Press.

Dubey, Y. P. (1985). *Information poverty: A third-world perspective.* ERIC document ED 314051.

Dudley, M. (2013). *Public libraries and resilient cities.* Chicago: American Library Association.

Duffy, T. M. (2001). Museums of "human suffering" and the struggle for human rights. *Museum International, 53*(1), 10–16.

DuMont, R. R. (1977). *Reform and reaction: The big city public library in American life.* Westport, CT: Greenwood.

Duran, D. F. (1978). Information status and the mass media: The case of the urban poor. *Collection Building, 1,* 49–60.

Durrani, S., & Smallwood, E. (2006). The professional is political: Redefining the social role of public libraries. *Progressive Librarian, 27,* 3–22.

Eberhart, G. (2013). The prescription for finding healthcare information. *American Libraries.* Available: http://www.americanlibrariesmagazine.org/blog/prescription-finding-healthcare-information

Edwards, J. B., & Edwards, S. P. (2010). *Beyond Article 19: Libraries and social and cultural rights.* Duluth, MN: Library Juice.

Engler, R. (2011). The toughest nut: Handling cases pitting unrepresented litigants against represented ones. *Juvenile and Family Court Journal, 62*(1), 10–31.

Ennis, P. H., & Fryden, F. N. (1960). The library in the community use studies revisited. *Library Quarterly, 30,* 253–265.

Enright, N. F. (2013). The violence of information literacy: Neoliberalism and the human as capital. In L. Gregory & S. Higgins (Eds.), *Information literacy and social justice* (pp. 15–38). Sacramento, CA: Library Juice.

Evans, T. (1998). Introduction: Power, hegemony, and the universalization of human rights. In T. Evans (Ed.), *Human rights fifty years on: A reappraisal* (pp. 2–21). Manchester, UK: Manchester University Press.

FCC. (2014b). *Modernizing the e-rate program for schools and libraries,* WC Docket No. 13-184, Second Report and Order and Order on Reconsideration, FCC 14–189 (rel. Dec. 19, 2014). Available: http://transition.fcc.gov/Daily_Releases/Daily_Business/2014/db1219/FCC-14-189A1.pdf

Federal Communications Commission (FCC). (2010). *The national broadband plan: Connecting America*. Washington, DC: Author. Available: http://www.broadband.gov/

Federal Communications Commission (FCC). (July 2014a). *FCC modernizes E-Rate program to expand robust wi-fi networks in the nation's schools and libraries*. Available: http://www.fcc.gov/document/fcc-modernizes-e-rate-expand-robust-wi-fi-schools-libraries

Fink, C., & Kenny, C. J. (2003). W(h)ither the digital divide? *Info, 5*, 15–24.

First, P. F., & Hart, Y. Y. (2002). Access to cyberspace: The new issue in educational justice. *Journal of Law & Education, 31*, 385–411.

Fisher, K., & Naumer, C. M. (2005). Information grounds: Theoretical basis and empirical findings on information flow in social settings. In A. Spink & C. Cole (Eds.), *New directions in human information behavior* (pp. 93–111). New York: Springer.

Floridi, L. (2002). On defining library and information science as applied philosophy of information. *Social Epistemology, 16*, 37–49.

Fox, S. (2004). *Older Americans and the Internet*. Washington, DC: Pew Research Center.

Fox, S., & Livingston, G. (2007). *Latinos online: Hispanics with lower levels of education and English proficiency remain largely disconnected from the Internet*. Washington, DC: Pew Research Center. Available: http://www.pewinternet.org

Fox, S., & Madden, M. (2005). *Generations online*. Washington, DC: Pew Research Center. Available: http://www.pewinternet.org

Frankena, W. E. (1962). The concept of social justice. In R. B. Brandt (Ed.), *Social justice* (pp. 1–30). Englewood Cliffs, NJ: Prentice Hall.

Fritschel, B. L. (2007). Trends in library collaboration to provide access to legal information. In National Center for State Courts, *Future trends in state courts 2007* (pp. 84–87). Available: http://cdm16501.contentdm.oclc.org/cdm/ref/collection/accessfair/id/129

Fuller, P. F. (1994). The politics of LSCA during the Reagan and Bush administrations: An analysis. *Library Quarterly, 64*, 294–318.

Gaffney, L. M. (2013). "Is your library family friendly?" Libraries as a site of conservative activism, 1992–2002. In C. Pawley & L. S. Robbins (Eds.), *Libraries and the reading public in twentieth-century America* (pp. 185–199). Madison: University of Wisconsin Press.

Galan, V. (2011). Partners in community enhancement. *American Libraries, 42*(3–4), 41.

Galanter, M. (2009). Access to justice in a world of expanding social capability. *Fordham Urban Law Journal, 37*(1), 115–128.

Galbraith, J. K. (1998). *Created unequal: The crisis in American pay*. New York: Free Press.

Gannett Center for Media Studies. (1987). *The cost of technology: Information prosperity and information poverty*. New York: Columbia University.

Garmer, A. K. (2014). *Rising to the challenge: Re-envisioning public libraries*. Aspen, CO: Aspen Institute.

Garoogian, R. (1991). Librarian/patron confidentiality: An ethical challenge. *Library Trends, 40*, 216–233.

Garrison, D. (1993). *Apostles of culture: The public librarian and American society, 1876–1920*. Madison: University of Wisconsin Press.

Gathegi, J. N. (2005). The public library and the (de)evolution of a legal doctrine. *Library Quarterly, 75*, 1–19.

Gehner, J. (2010). Libraries, low-income people, and social exclusion. *Public Library Quarterly, 29*(1), 39–47.

Geller, E. (1974). Intellectual freedom: Eternal principle or unanticipated consequence? *Library Journal, 99*, 1364–1367.

Geller, E. (1984). *Forbidden books in American public libraries, 1876–1939: A study in cultural change*. Westport, CT: Greenwood.

Good, J. (2006–2007). The hottest place in hell: The crisis of neutrality in contemporary librarianship. *Progressive Librarian, 28*, 25–29.

Goodman, R., Jinks, D., & Woods, A. K. (2012). Introduction: Social science and human rights. In R. Goodman, D. Jinks, & A. K. Woods (Eds.), *Understanding social action, promoting human rights* (pp. 3–22). Oxford: Oxford University Press.

Gorham, U., Bertot, J. C., Jaeger, P. T., & Taylor, N. G. (2013). E-government success in public libraries: Library and government agency partnerships delivering services to new immigrants. In J. Ramon Gil-Garcia (Ed.), *E-government success around the world: Cases, empirical studies , and practical recommendations* (pp. 41–59). Hershey, PA: IGI Global.

Gorham-Oscilowski, U., & Jaeger, P. T. (2008). National security letters, the USA PATRIOT Act, and the Constitution: The tensions between national security and civil rights. *Government Information Quarterly, 25*, 625–644.

Governing. (2014). *Governing data: State and local government employment monthly data.* Available: http://www.governing.com/gov-data/public-workforce-salaries/monthly-government-employment-changes-totals.html

Graham, J. B. (2003). Now's not the time to be neutral? The myth and reality of the library as neutral entity. *Alabama Librarian, 53*(2), 9–11.

Graham, P. T. (2001). Public librarians and the civil rights movement. *Library Quarterly, 71*, 1–27.

Granovetter, M. S. (1973). The strength of weak ties. *American Journal of Sociology, 78*, 1360–1380.

Granovetter, M. S. (1983). The strength of weak ties: A network theory revisited. *Sociological Theory, 1*, 201–233.

Greenberg, B. S., & Dervin, B. L. (1970a). Mass communication among the urban poor. *Public Opinion Quarterly, 34*, 224–235.

Greenberg, B. S., & Dervin, B. L. (1970b). *Use of the mass media by the urban poor: Findings of three research projects, with an annotated bibliography.* New York: Praeger.

Greenstein, R., & Esterhuysen, A. (2012). The right to development in the information society. In R. F. Jorgensen (Ed.), *Human rights in the global information society* (pp. 281–302). Cambridge, MA: MIT Press.

Gregory, L., & Higgins, S. (Eds.). (2013). *Information literacy and social justice: Radical professional praxis.* Sacramento, CA: Library Juice.

Gurstein, M. (2003). Effective use: A community informatics strategy beyond the digital divide. *First Monday , 8*(12). Available: http://firstmonday.org/ojs/fm/article/view/1798/1678

Hafner, A. W. (1987). Public libraries and society in the information age. *Reference Librarian, 18*, 107–118.

Hale-Janeke, A., & Blackburn, S. (2008). Law librarians and the self-represented litigant. *Legal Reference Services Quarterly, 27*(1), 65–88.

Hall, R. A. (2009). Exploring the core: An examination of required courses in ALA-accredited. *Education for Information, 27*(1), 57–67.

Halpin, E. F., Hick, S., & Hoskins, E. (2000). Introduction. In S. Hick, E. F. Halpin, & E. Hoskins (Eds.), *Human rights and the Internet* (pp. 3–15). New York: St. Martin's.

Halsey, R. S. (2003). *Lobbying for public and school libraries: A history and political playbook.* Lanham, MD: Scarecrow.

Hamelink, C. (1994). *The politics of world communication: A human rights perspective.* London: Sage.

Hanks, D. (2014, September 9). Miami-Dade libraries need to end "bookish" attitude, panel says. *Miami Herald.* 9. Available: http://www.miamiherald.com/news/local/community/miami-dade/article2309893.html

Hanley, R. (1998, June 29). Jersey City librarians protest plan for private contractor. *New York Times*, pp. B1, B6.

Hannaford-Agor, P., & Mott, N. (2003). Research on self-represented litigation: Preliminary results and methodological considerations. *Justice System Journal, 24*(2), 163–181.

Hargittai, E., & Walejko, G. (2008). The participation divide: Content creation and sharing in the digital age. *Information, Communication & Society, 11*(2), 239–256.

Harris, M. H. (1973). The purpose of the American public library: A revisionist interpretation of history. *Library Journal, 98*, 2509–2514.

Harris, M. H. (1976). Public libraries and the decline of the democratic dogma. *Library Journal, 101*, 2225–2230.

Hartford Public Library. (2013). *2013 annual report.* Available: http://hplct.org/assets/uploads/files/about/Annual%20Report/AR%20HPL_for%20website_10_24_13.pdf

Harvey, D. (2007a). Neoliberalism and the city. *Studies in Social Justice, 1*, 2–13.

Harvey, D. (2007b). Neoliberalism as creative destruction. *Annals of the American Academy of Political and Social Science, 610*, 22–44.

Hastings, S. K. (2015). If diversity is a natural state, why don't our libraries mirror the populations they serve? *Library Quarterly, 85*, 133–138.

Heckart, R. J. (1991). The library as marketplace of ideas. *College and Research Libraries, 52*, 491–505.

Hendry, J. D. (2000). Social inclusion and the information poor. *Library Review, 49*(7), 331–336.

Henry, M., Cortes, A., & Morris, S. (2013). *The 2013 Annual Homeless Assessment Report (AHAR) to Congress.* The U.S. Department of Housing and Urban Development Office of Community Planning and Development. Available: https://www.onecpd.info/resources/documents/ahar-2013-part1.pdf

Herdman, M. M. (1943). The public library in the Depression. *Library Quarterly, 13*, 310–334.

Herndon, T., Ash, M., & Pollin, R. (2013). *Does high public debt consistently stifle economic growth? A critique of Reinhart and Rogoff.* Amherst, MA: Political Economic Research Institute.

Hoffman, M. (2001). Developing the electronic collection: The University of Minnesota Human Rights Library. *Legal Reference Services Quarterly, 19*, 143–155.

Hornick, R. C. (2012). Why can't we sell human rights like we sell soap? In R. Goodman, D. Jinks, & A. K. Woods (Eds.), *Understanding social action, promoting human rights* (pp. 47–69). Oxford: Oxford University Press.

Horrigan, J. B. (2009). *Obama's online opportunities II: If you build it, will they log on?* Washington, DC: Pew Research Center. Available: http://www.pewinternet.org/~/media//Files/Reports/2009/PIP_Broadband percent20Barriers.pdf

Horrigan, J. B., & Rainie, L. (2002a). *Counting on the Internet.* Washington, DC: Pew Research Center. Available: http://www.pewinternet.org/

Horrigan, J. B., & Rainie, L. (2002b). *Getting serious online.* Washington, DC: Pew Research Center. Available: http://www.pewinternet.org/

Houseman, A. W. (2001). Civil legal assistance for low-income persons: Looking back and looking forward. *Fordham Urban Law Journal, 29*(3), 1213–1243.

Human Rights Council. (2011). *Report of the Special Rapporteur on the promotion and protection of the right to freedom of opinion and expression, Frank La Rue.* United Nations. Available: http://www.un.org

Hummel, P. (2012). Library advocacy in hard times. *OLA Quarterly, 18*(2), 4–5.

Hussain, A. (2000). Preface. In S. Hick, E. F. Halpin, & E. Hoskins (Eds.), *Human rights and the Internet* (pp. x–xii). New York: St. Martin's.

Hussey, L. K., & Velasquez, D. L. (2011). Forced advocacy: How communities respond to library budget cuts. *Advances in Librarianship, 34*, 59–93.

Ignatieff, M. (2005). Introduction: American expectionalism and human rights. In M. Ignatieff (Ed.), *American exceptionalism and human rights* (pp. 1–26). Princeton, NJ: Princeton University Press.

Imhoff, K. R. T. (2006). Creating advocates for public libraries. *Public Library Quarterly, 25*(1–2), 155–170.

International Federation of Library Associations and Institutions (IFLA) & United Nations Educational, Scientific and Cultural Organization (UNESCO). (1994). *Public library manifesto.* Last updated June 18, 2014. Available: http://www.ifla.org/publications/iflaunesco-public-library-manifesto-1994

International Federation of Library Associations and Institutions (IFLA) & United Nations Educational, Scientific and Cultural Organization (UNESCO). (2008). *Multicultural library manifesto.* Last updated September 4, 2014. Available: http://www.ifla.org/publications/node/632

Jackson, B. (2005). The conceptual history of social justice. *Political Studies Review, 3*, 356–373.

Jacobs, H. L. M., & Berg, S. (2011). Reconnecting information literacy policy with the core values of librarianship. *Library Trends, 60*(2), 383–394.

Jacobs, J. A., Jacobs, J. R., & Yeo, S. (2005). Government information in the digital age: The once and future Federal Depository Library Program. *Journal of Academic Librarianship, 31*(3), 198–208.

Jaeger, P. T. (2008). Building e-government into the library and information science curriculum: The future of government information and services. *Journal of Education for Library and Information Science , 49,* 167–179.

Jaeger, P. T. (2012). *Disability and the Internet: Confronting a digital divide.* Boulder, CO: Lynne Rienner.

Jaeger, P. T. (2013). Internet justice: Reconceptualizing the legal rights of persons with disabilities to promote equal access in the age of rapid technological change. *Review of Disability Studies, 9*(1), 39–59.

Jaeger, P. T., & Bertot, J. C. (2010). Transparency and technological change: Ensuring equal and sustained public access to government information. *Government Information Quarterly, 27,* 371–376.

Jaeger, P. T., & Bertot, J. C. (2011). Responsibility rolls down: Public libraries and the social and policy obligations of ensuring access to e-government and government information. *Public Library Quarterly, 30*(2), 91–116.

Jaeger, P. T., Bertot, J. C., & Gorham, U. (2013). Wake up the nation: Public libraries, policymaking, and political discourse. *Library Quarterly, 83,* 61–72.

Jaeger, P. T., Bertot, J. C., Kodama, C. M., Katz, S. M., & DeCoster, E. J. (2011). Describing and measuring the value of public libraries: The growth of the Internet and the evolution of library value. *First Monday, 11*(7). Available: http://www.uic.edu/htbin/cgiwrap/bin/ojs/index.php/fm/article/viewArticle/3765/3074

Jaeger, P. T., Bertot, J. C., & McClure, C. R. (2003). The impact of the USA PATRIOT Act on collection and analysis of personal information under the Foreign Intelligence Surveillance Act. *Government Information Quarterly, 20*(3), 295–314.

Jaeger, P. T., Bertot, J. C., & McClure, C. R. (2004). The effects of the Children's Internet Protection Act (CIPA) in public libraries and its implications for research: A statistical, policy, and legal analysis. *Journal of the American Society for Information Science and Technology, 55*(13), 1131–1139.

Jaeger, P. T., Bertot, J. C., McClure, C. R., & Langa, L. A. (2006). The policy implications of Internet connectivity in public libraries. *Government Information Quarterly, 23*(1), 123–141.

Jaeger, P. T., Bertot, J. C., McClure, C. R., & Rodriguez, M. (2007). Public libraries and Internet access across the United States: A comparison by state 2004–2006. *Information Technology & Libraries, 26*(2), 4–14.

Jaeger, P. T., Bertot, J. C., & Shuler, J. A. (2010). The Federal Depository Library Program (FDLP), academic libraries, and access to government information. *Journal of Academic Librarianship, 36,* 469–478.

Jaeger, P. T., Bertot, J. C., & Subramaniam, M. (2013). Preparing future librarians to effectively serve their communities. *Library Quarterly, 83,* 243–248.

Jaeger, P. T., Bertot, J. C., Thompson, K. M., Katz, S. M., & DeCoster, E. J. (2012). Digital divides, digital literacy, digital inclusion, and public libraries: The intersection of public policy and public access. *Public Library Quarterly, 31*(1), 1–20.

Jaeger, P. T., & Bowman, C. A. (2005). *Understanding disability: Inclusion, access, diversity, and civil rights.* Westport, CT: Praeger.

Jaeger, P. T., & Burnett, G. (2005). Information access and exchange among small worlds in a democratic society: The role of policy in redefining information behavior in the post-9/11 United States. *Library Quarterly, 75*(4), 464–495.

Jaeger, P. T., & Burnett, G. (2010). *Information worlds: Social context, technology, and information behavior in the age of the Internet.* New York: Routledge.

Jaeger, P. T., Cooke, N., Feltis, C., Hamiel, M., Jardine, F., & Shilton, K. (2015). The virtuous circle revisited: Injecting diversity and inclusion into LIS from education to advocacy. *Library Quarterly, 85,* 150–171.

Jaeger, P. T., & Fleischmann, K. R. (2007). Public libraries, values, trust, and e-government. *Information Technology & Libraries , 26*(4), 34–43.

Jaeger, P. T., Gorham, U., Bertot, J. C., & Sarin, L. C. (2014). *Public libraries, public policies, and political processes: Serving and transforming communities in times of economic and political constraint.* Lanham, MD: Rowman & Littlefield.

Jaeger, P. T., Gorham, U., Sarin, L. C., & Bertot, J. C. (2013). Democracy, neutrality, and value demonstration in the age of austerity, *Library Quarterly, 83*, 368–382.

Jaeger, P. T., & McClure, C. R. (2004). Potential legal challenges to the application of the Children's Internet Protection Act (CIPA) in public libraries: Strategies and issues. *First Monday, 9*(2). Available: http://www.firstmonday.org/issues/issue9_2/jaeger/index.html

Jaeger, P. T., McClure, C. R., & Bertot, J. C. (2005). The E-Rate program and libraries and library consortia, 2000–2004: Trends and issues. *Information Technology & Libraries, 24*(2), 57–67.

Jaeger, P. T., McClure, C. R., Bertot, J. C., & Langa, L. A. (2005). CIPA: Decisions, implementation, and impacts. *Public Libraries, 44*(2), 105–109.

Jaeger, P. T., McClure, C. R., Bertot, J. C., & Snead, J. T. (2004). The USA PATRIOT Act, the Foreign Intelligence Surveillance Act, and information policy research in libraries: Issues, impacts, and questions for library researchers. *Library Quarterly, 74*(2), 99–121.

Jaeger, P. T., Sarin, L. C., Gorham, U., & Bertot, J. C. (2013). Libraries, policy, and politics in a democracy: The four historical epochs. *Library Quarterly, 83*, 166–181.

Jaeger, P. T., Taylor, N. G., Bertot, J. C., Perkins, N., & Wahl, E. E. (2012). The co-evolution of e-government and public libraries: Technologies, access, education, and partnerships. *Library & Information Science Research, 34*, 271–281.

Jaeger, P. T., Taylor, N. G., Gorham, U., Kettnich, K., Sarin, L. C., & Peterson, K. (2014). Library research and what libraries actually do now: Education, inclusion, social services, public spaces, digital literacy, social justice, human rights, and other community needs. *Library Quarterly, 84*(4), 491–493.

Jaeger, P. T., & Thompson, K. M. (2003). E-government around the world: Lessons, challenges, and new directions. *Government Information Quarterly, 20*(4), 389–394.

Jaeger, P. T., & Thompson, K. M. (2004). Social information behavior and the democratic process: Information poverty, normative behavior, and electronic government in the United States. *Library & Information Science Research, 26*(1), 94–107.

Jaeger, P. T., & Yan, Z. (2009). One law with two outcomes: Comparing the implementation of the Children's Internet Protection Act in public libraries and public schools. *Information Technology & Libraries, 28*(1), 8–16.

Jakowska, M. A., Smith, B. J., & Buehler, M. A. (2014). Engagement of academic libraries and information science schools in creating curriculum for sustainability. *Journal of Academic Librarianship, 40*, 45–54.

James, S. E. (1986). Economic hard times and public library use: A close look at the librarian's axiom. *Public Library Quarterly, 7*(3–4), 61–70.

Jerrard, J., Bolt, N., & Strege, K. (2012). *Privatizing libraries.* Chicago: American Library Association.

Joeckel, J. B. (1932). Supply and demand in the library profession. *Library Journal, 37*, 103–110.

Johnson, B. S. (1989). A more cooperative clerk: The confidentiality of library records. *Law Library Journal, 81*, 769–802.

Johnson, R. G., III. (Ed.). (2009). *A twenty-first century approach to teaching social justice: Educating for both advocacy and action.* New York: Peter Lang.

Jones, P. A., Jr. (1999). *Libraries, immigrants, and the American experience.* Westport, CT: Greenwood.

Jordan, P. (1975). Librarians and social commitment. *Assistant Librarian, 68*(4), 62–66.

Jorgensen, R. F. (2006a). *Human rights in the global information society.* Cambridge, MA: MIT Press.

Jorgensen, R. F. (2006b). The right to express oneself and seek information. In R. F. Jorgensen (Ed.), *Human rights in the global information society* (pp. 53–72). Cambridge, MA: MIT Press.

Jue, D. K., Koontz, C. M., Magpantay, J. A., Lance, K. C., & Seidl, A. M. (1999). Using public libraries to provide technology access for individuals in poverty: A national analysis of library market areas using a geographic information system. *Library & Information Science Research, 21*, 299–325.

Kennedy, B. M. (1989). Confidentiality of library records: A survey of problems, policies, and laws. *Law Library Journal, 81*, 733–767.

Kent, S. G. (1996). American public libraries: A long transformation. *Daedalus, 125*(4), 207–220.

Kerslake, E., & Kinnell, M. (1998). Public libraries, public interest and the information society: Theoretical issues in the social impact of public libraries. *Journal of Librarianship and Information Science, 30*(3), 159–167.

Klick, L. R. (2011). Uncommon services: Public library services to incarcerated populations. *InterActions: UCLA Journal of Education and Information Studies, 7*(1). Available: http://escholarship.org/uc/item/760020nf

Klinefelter, A. (2003). The role of librarians in challenges to the USA PATRIOT Act. *North Carolina Journal of Law & Technology, 5*, 219–226.

Klinefelter, A. (2007). Privacy and library public services: Or, I know what you read last summer. *Legal Reference Services Quarterly, 26*(1–2), 253–279.

Kniffel, L. (2002). Who wants to be the first to go to jail? *American Libraries, 33*(7), 46.

Kniffel, L. (2005). From cradle to grave: A lifetime in libraries. *American Libraries, 36*(8), 33.

Kniffel, L. (2010, October 17). Libraries now more than ever. *American Libraries*. Available: http://www.americanlibrariesmagazine.org/article/libraries-now-more-ever

Knox, E. (2013). The challengers of West Bend: The library as a community institution. In C. Pawley & L. S. Robbins (Eds.), *Libraries and the reading public in twentieth-century America* (pp. 200–213). Madison: University of Wisconsin Press.

Koepfler, J., Mascaro, C., & Jaeger, P. T. (2014). Homelessness, wirelessness, and (in)visibility. *First Monday, 19*(3). Available: http://firstmonday.org/ojs/fm/article/view/4748/3729

Kommers, N., & Rainie, L. (2002). *Use of the Internet at major life moments.* Washington, DC: Pew Research Center. Available: http://www.pewinternet.org/

Kramp, R. S. (1975/2010). *The Great Depression: Its impact on forty-six large American public libraries.* Duluth, MN: Library Juice.

Kranich, N. (Ed.). (2001). *Libraries and democracy: The cornerstones of liberty.* Chicago: American Library Association.

Labaree, D. F. (1997). Public goods, private goods: The American struggle over educational goals. *American Educational Research Journal, 34*(1), 39–81.

Landsman, S. (2009). The growing challenge of pro se litigation. *Lewis & Clark Law Review, 13*(2), 439–460.

Lang, J. P. (Ed.) (1988). *Unequal access to information resources: Problems and needs of the world's information poor.* Ann Arbor, MI: Pierian Press.

Larsen, E., & Rainie, L. (2002). *The rise of the e-citizen: How people use government agencies' websites.* Washington, DC: Pew Research Center.

Larson, K. C. (2001). The Saturday Evening Girls: A Progressive Era library club and the intellectual life of working class and immigrant girls in turn-of-the-century Boston. *Library Quarterly, 71*, 195–230.

Lauren, P. G. (2011). *The evolution of international human rights: Visions seen* (3rd ed.). Philadelphia: University of Pennsylvania Press.

Lazer, D. (2012). Networks and politics: The case of human rights. In R. Goodman, D. Jinks, & A. K. Woods (Eds.), *Understanding social action, promoting human rights* (pp. 244–264). Oxford: Oxford University Press.

Leckie, G. J., & Buschman, J. E. (2007). Space, place, and libraries: An introduction. In J. E. Buschman & G. J. Leckie (Eds.), *The library as place: History, community, and culture* (pp. 3–25). Westport, CT: Libraries Unlimited.

Legal Services Corporation (LSC). (2012, October). *Report of the Pro Bono Task Force.* Available: http://www.lsc.gov/sites/default/files/LSC/lscgov4/PBTF_%20Report_FINAL.pdf

Leigh, R. D. (1950). *The public library in the United States: The general report of the Public Library Inquiry.* New York: Columbia.

Leigh, R. D. (1957). Changing concepts of the public library's role. *Library Quarterly, 27,* 223–234.

Lerner, F. (2009). *The story of libraries: From the invention of writing to the computer age.* New York: Continuum.

Leubsdorf, B. (2014, September 4). Fed: Gap between rich, poor Americans widened during recovery. *Wall Street Journal.* Available: http://online.wsj.com/articles/fed-gap-between-rich-poor-americans-widened-during-recovery-1409853628

Lewis, O. (1959). *Five families: Mexican case studies in the culture of poverty.* New York: Basic.

Lewis, O. (1961). *The children of Sánchez: Autobiography of a Mexican family.* New York: Random House.

Library Copyright Alliance. (2007). *Library Copyright Alliance statement on copyright reform.* Available: http://www.librarycopyrightalliance.org

Lievrouw, L., & Farb, S. (2003). Information and equity. *Annual Review of Information Science and Technology, 37,* 499–540.

Likosky, M. B. (2006). *Law, infrastructure, and human rights.* New York: Cambridge.

Lilienthal, S. M. (2011, June 15). The problem is not the homeless. *Library Journal,* pp. 30–34.

Lilienthal, S. M. (2013, February 4). Prison and libraries: Public service inside and out. *Library Journal.* Available: http://lj.libraryjournal.com/2013/02/library-services/prison-and-public-libraries/

Lindsay, A. (2001). Archives and justice: Willard Ireland's contribution to the changing legal framework of aboriginal rights in Canada, 1963–1973. *Archivaria, 71,* 35–62.

Lingel, J. (2012). Occupy Wall Street and the myth of technological death of the library. *First Monday, 17*(8). Available: http://firstmonday.org/ojs/index.php/fm/article/view/3845/3280

Livingston, G. (2010). *The Latino digital divide: The native born versus the foreign born.* Washington, DC: Pew Research Center. Available: http://www.pewinternet.org

Lowery, W., & Hernandez, A. (2014, October 14). In Ferguson, coordinated disobedience. *Washington Post,* p. A2.

Lukenbill, W. B. (2006). Helping youth at risk: An overview of reformist movements in public libraries to youth. *New Review of Children's Literature and Librarianship, 12,* 197–213.

Lynch, M. J. (2002). Economic hard times and public library use revisited. *American Libraries, 33*(7), 62–63.

Lyon Declaration on Access to Information and Development. (2014). Available: http://lyondeclaration.org

Lyons, L. (2011). Human rights: A universal declaration. *College & Research Library News, 72*(5), 290–293.

MacCann, D. (1989). *Social responsibility in librarianship: Essays on equality.* Jefferson, NC: McFarland.

Machlup, F. (1962). *The production and distribution of knowledge in the United States.* Princeton, NJ: Princeton University Press.

Mackenzie, A. (2010). *Wirelessness: Radical empiricism in network cultures.* Cambridge, MA: MIT Press.

Mandel, L. H., Bishop, B. W., McClure, C. R., Bertot, J. C., & Jaeger, P. T. (2010). Broadband for public libraries: Importance, issues, and research needs. *Government Information Quarterly, 27,* 280–291.

Maness, J. M. (2006). Library 2.0 theory: Web 2.0 and its implications for libraries. *Webology, 3*(2). Available: http://webology.org/2006/v3n2/a25.html

Mann, H. (1952). *Twelfth annual report: Covering the year 1848.* The Horace Mann League Addition. Available: http://www.hmleague.org

"Manufacturing Makerspaces." (2013, February 6). *American Libraries.* Available: http://www.americanlibrariesmagazine.org/article/manufacturing-makerspaces

Markey, K. (2004). Current educational trends in the information and library science curriculum. *Journal of Education for Library and Information Science, 45*(4), 317–339.

Mars, A. (2013, April 26). Library service to the homeless. *Public libraries Online.* Available: http://publiclibrariesonline.org/2013/04/library-service-to-the-homeless/

Mart, S. N. (2003). The right to receive information. *Law Library Journal, 95,* 175–189.

Martin, K. (2002). The USA PATRIOT Act's application to library patron records. *Journal of Legislation, 29*, 283–306.

Martin, R. S. (2000). *The impact of outsourcing and privatization on library services and management: A study for the American Library Association.* Denton, TX: Texas Woman's University.

Martin, R. S., Blalock, L., Wells, G., & Wolf, M. T. (2006). Engaging your community: Libraries as place. In B. Bernhardt, T. Daniels, K. Steinle, and K. P. Strauch (Eds.), *Charleston Conference Proceedings 2005* (pp. 188–202). Westport, CT: Libraries Unlimited.

Martins, C., & Martins, S. (2005, May/June). The impact of the USA PATRIOT Act on record management. *Information Management Journal*, pp. 52–58.

Mason. R. O. (1986). Four ethical issues of the information age. *MIS Quarterly, 10*(1), 5–12.

Mathiesen, K. (2012). The human right to Internet access: A philosophical defense. *International Review of Information Ethics, 18*. Available: http://www.i-r-i-e.net/inhalt/018/Mathiesen.pdf

Mathiesen, K. (2013). The human right to a public library. *Journal of Information Ethics, 22*, 60–79.

Mathiesen, K. (2014a). Facets of access: A conceptual and standard threats analysis. *iConference 2014 Proceedings*, 605–614.

Mathiesen, K. (2014b). Human rights for the digital age. *Journal of Mass Media Ethics, 29*, 2–18.

Matz, C. (2008). Libraries and the USA PATRIOT Act: Values in conflict. *Journal of Library Administration, 47*(3–4), 69–87.

McClure, D. (1974). *The cost of poverty: Information for action.* Frankfort, KY: Legislative Research Commission.

McCook, K. d. l. P. (2000). *A place at the table: Participating in community building.* Chicago: American Library Association.

McCook, K. d. l. P. (2002, May). Rocks in the whirlpool. *American Library Association.* Available: http://www.ala.org/aboutala/missionhistory/keyactionareas/equityaction/rockswhirlpool#tca

McCook, K. d. l. P. (2004). Public libraries and people in jail. *Reference & User Services Quarterly, 44*(1), 26–30.

McCook, K. d. l. P. (2007). Librarians as advocates for the human rights of immigrants. *Progressive Librarian, 29*, 50–53.

McCook, K. d. l. P. (2011). *Introduction to public librarianship* (2nd ed.). New York: Neal Schuman.

McCook, K. d. l. P. (2014). Librarians as Wikipedians: From library history to librarianship and human rights. *Progressive Librarian, 42*, 60–80.

McCook, K. d. l. P., & Phenix, K. J. (2006). Public libraries and human rights. *Public Library Quarterly, 25*, 57–73.

McCreadie, M., & Rice, R. E. (1999). Trends in analyzing access to information, part I: Cross-disciplinary conceptions of access. *Information Processing and Management, 35*, 45–76.

McCrossen, A. (2006). "One more cathedral" or "mere lounging places for bummers?" The cultural politics of leisure and the public library in Gilded Age America. *Libraries & the Cultural Record, 41*, 169–188.

McDowell, K. (2010). Which truth, what fiction? Librarians' book recommendations for children, 1877–1890. In A. R. Nelson & J. L. Rudolph (Eds.), *Education and the culture of print in modern America* (pp. 15–35). Madison: University of Wisconsin Press.

McDowell, K. (2011). Children's voices in librarians' words, 1890–1930. *Libraries & the Cultural Record, 46*, 73–100.

Mchombu, K. J. (2004). *Sharing knowledge for community development and transformation.* Ottawa: Oxfam Canada.

McIver, W. J., Birdsall, W. F., & Rasmussen, M. (2003). The Internet and the right to communicate. *First Monday, 8*(2). Available: http://firstmonday.org/ojs/fm/article/view/1102/1022

McKinney, D. (2012). *The man who saw a ghost: The life and work of Henry Fonda.* New York: St. Martin's.

McMenemy, D. (2007). Librarians and ethical neutrality: Revisiting *The Creed of a Librarian*. *Library Review, 56*, 177–181.

Mehra, B., Rioux, K. S., & Albright, K. S. (2009). Social justice in library and information science. In *Encyclopedia of library and information science* (pp. 4820–4836). New York: Taylor & Francis.

Mehra, B., & Srinivasan, R. (2007). The library-community convergence framework for community action: Libraries as catalysts for social change. *Libri, 57*, 123–139.

Menou, M. J. (1983). Mini- and micro-computers and the eradication of information poverty in the less developed countries. In C. Keren & L. Perlmutter (Eds.). *The application of mini- and micro-computers in information, documentation and libraries* (pp. 359–366). North Holland: Elsevier Science.

Mestre, L. (2010). *Librarians serving diverse populations: Challenges and opportunities.* Chicago: American Library Association.

Miami Herald. (2014, October 12). With no Internet at home, kids crowd libraries for online homework. *Miami Herald.* Available: http://www.tcmnet.com/usubmit/2014/10/12/8063284.htm

Miles, S. A. (1967, fall). An introduction to the vocabulary of information technology. *Technical Communications*, pp. 20–24.

Miller, C., Zickuhr, K., Rainie, L., & Purcell, K. (2013). *Parents, children, libraries, and reading.* Washington, DC: Pew Research Center. Available: http://libraries.pewinternet.org/2013/05/01/parents-children-libraries-and-reading/

Miller, M. (1993). Midwinter by the numbers: Important issues and events of ALA's Denver meeting came with call numbers. *American Libraries, 24*(3), 222–230.

Montgomery, B. P. (1996). Archiving human rights: A paradigm for collection development. *Journal of Academic Librarianship, 22*, 87–96.

Moore, M. (1995). *Creating public value: Strategic management in government.* Cambridge, MA: Harvard University Press.

Moore, M., & Khagram, S. (2004). *On creating public value: What business might learn from government about strategic management* [Corporate Social Responsibility Initiative Working Paper No. 3]. Cambridge, MA: Harvard University Press.

Moravcsik, A. (2005). The paradox of U.S. human rights policy. In M. Ignatieff (Ed.), *American exceptionalism and human rights* (pp. 147–197). Princeton, NJ: Princeton University Press.

Morrone, Melissa (Ed.). (2014). *Informed agitation: Library and information skills in social justice movements and beyond.* Sacramento, CA: Library Juice.

Mossberger, K., Tolbert, C. J., & McNeal, R. S. (2008). *Digital citizenship: The Internet, society, and participation.* Cambridge, MA: MIT Press.

Mossberger, K., Tolbert, C. J., & Stansbury, M. (2003). *Virtual inequality: Beyond the digital divide.* Washington, DC: Georgetown University Press.

Moyn, S. (2012, May 12). Human rights, not so pure anymore. *New York Times.* Available: http://www.nytimes.com

Muggleton, T. H. (2013). Public libraries and difficulties with targeting the homeless. *Library Review, 62*(1–2), 7–18.

Murdock, G., & Golding, P. (1989). Information poverty and political inequality: Citizenship in the age of privatized communications. *Journal of Communication, 39*(3), 180–195.

Musman, K. (1993). *Technological innovations in libraries, 1860–1960.* Westport, CT: Greenwood.

Nash, K. (2009). *The cultural politics of human rights: Comparing the US and the UK.* New York: Cambridge.

Nath, V. (2001). *Heralding ICT enabled knowledge societies: Way forward for the developing countries.* Available: http://www.cddc.vt.edu/knownet/articles/heralding.htm

National Center for Education Statistics. (2003). Demographics—Overall. *National Assessment of Adult Literacy (NAAL).* Available: http://nces.ed.gov/naal/kf_demographics.asp

National Center for State Courts (NCSC). (2006). Access to justice: The self-represented litigant. In National Center for State Courts, *Future Trends in State Courts 2006* (pp. 18–19). Available: http://ncsc.contentdm.oclc.org/cdm/singleitem/collection/accessfair/id/135

National Center for State Courts (NCSC). (2012). *Access brief 1: Self-help services.* Available: http://cdm16501.contentdm.oclc.org/utils/getfile/collection/accessfair/id/263/filename/264.pdf

National Telecommunications and Information Administration. (NTIA). (n.d.). *State broadband initiative.* Available: http://www.ntia.doc.gov/category/state-broadband-initiative

National Telecommunications and Information Administration (NTIA). (1995). *Falling through the net: A survey of the "have nots" in rural and urban America.* Washington, DC: Author.

National Telecommunications and Information Administration (NTIA). (1998). *Falling through the net II: New data on the digital divide.* Washington, DC: Author.

National Telecommunications and Information Administration (NTIA). (1999). *Falling through the net: Defining the digital divide.* Washington, DC: Author.

National Telecommunications and Information Administration (NTIA). (2000). *Falling through the net: Toward digital inclusion.* Washington, DC: Author.

National Telecommunications and Information Administration (NTIA). (2002). *A nation online: How Americans are expanding their use of the Internet.* Washington, DC: Author.

National Telecommunications and Information Administration (NTIA). (2014). *Broadband Technology Opportunities Program (BTOP) quarterly program status report.* Washington, DC: Author.

Nelson, J. A. (2006). Marketing and advocacy: Collaboration in principle and practice. *Public Library Quarterly, 25*(1–2), 117–135.

Newman, J. (2007). Re-mapping the public: Public libraries and the public sphere. *Cultural Studies, 21,* 887–909.

New York Comprehensive Center. (2011). *Information brief: Impact of school libraries on student achievement.* New York: Author.

Nicholas, K. (2003). Geo-policy barriers and rural Internet access: The regulatory role in constructing the digital divide. *Information Society, 19,* 287–295.

Nieto, S. (2010). Foreword. In T. K. Chapman & N. Hobbel (Eds.), *Social justice pedagogy across the curriculum: The practice of freedom* (pp. ix–x). New York: Routledge.

Norris, P. (2001). *Digital divide: Civic engagement, information poverty, and the Internet worldwide.* Cambridge: Cambridge University Press.

Nyquist, E. B. (1968). Poverty, prejudice, and the public library. *Library Quarterly, 38,* 78–89.

Oakland Public Library. (2014). *Second start adult literacy program.* Available: http://oaklandlibrary.org/services/second-start-adult-literacy-program

Oakleaf, M. J., Association of College and Research Libraries, & American Library Association. (2010). *The value of academic libraries: A comprehensive research review and report.* Chicago: Association of College and Research Libraries and American Library Association.

Olivarez-Giles, N. (2011, June 3). United Nations report: Internet access is a human right. *Los Angeles Times.* Available: http://www.latimes.com/business/technology

Oltmann, S. M. (2009). Information access: Toward a more robust conceptualization. *Proceedings of the American Society for Information Science and Technology, 46*(1), 1–17.

O'Neil, D. V., & Baker, P. M. A. (2003). The role of institutional motivations in technological adoption: Implementation of DeKalb County's Family Technology Resource Centers. *Information Society, 19,* 305–324.

Orman, L. (1987). Information intensive modeling. *MIS Quarterly, 11*(1), 73–84.

Pagels, E. (1979). Human rights: Legitimizing a recent concept. *Annals of the American Academy of Political Science, 442,* 57–62.

Park, J. C. (1980). Preachers, politics, and public education: A review of right-wing pressures against public schooling in America. *Phi Delta Kappan, 61*(9), 608–612.

Parker, E. B., & Dunn, D. A. (1972). Information technology: Its social potential. *Science, 176*(4042), 1392–1399.

Parker, R., Kaufman-Scarborough, C., & Parker, J. C. (2007). Libraries in transition to a marketing orientation: Are librarians' attitudes a barrier? *International Journal of Nonprofit and Voluntary Sector Marketing, 12,* 320–337.

Pateman, J., & Vincent, J. (2010). *Public libraries and social justice.* Surrey, UK: Ashgate.

Perlstein, R. (2008). *Nixonland: The rise of a president and the fracturing of America*. New York: Scribner.

Peterson, A. (2014, May 16). Why the death of net neutrality would be a disaster for libraries. *Washington Post*. Available: http://www.washingtonpost.com/blogs/the-switch/wp/2014/05/16/why-the-death-of-net-neurality-would-be-a-disaster-for-libraries

Pettinato, T. R. (2007). Legal information, the informed citizen, and the FDLP: The role of academic law librarians in promoting democracy. *Law Library Journal, 99*, 695–716.

Pettinato, T. R. (2008). Dealing with pro se patrons. *Public Services Quarterly, 4*(3), 283–289.

Pew Research Center. (2014, March). *Millennials in adulthood: Detached from institutions, networked with friends*. Available: http://www.pewsocialtrends.org/files/2014/03/2014-03-07_generations-report-version-for-web.pdf

Phenix, K. J., & McCook, K. d. l. P. (2005). Human rights and librarians. *Reference & User Services Quarterly, 45*, 23–26.

Poe, J. (2006). Information and referral services: A brief history. *Southeastern Librarian, 54*(1), 36–41.

Pogge, T. (2005). World poverty and human rights. *Ethics & International Affairs, 19*, 1–7.

Pomerantz, J., & Marchionini, G. (2007). The digital library as place. *Journal of Documentation, 63*, 505–533.

Potter, A. B. (2006). Zones of silence: A framework beyond the digital divide. *First Monday, 11*(5). Available: http://firstmonday.org/ojs/index.php/fm/article/view/1327/1247

Powell, A., Byrne, A., & Dailey, D. (2010). The essential Internet: Digital exclusion in low-income American communities. *Policy and Internet, 2*(2), article 7.

Preer, J. (2008). Promoting citizenship: How librarians helped get out the vote in the 1952 presidential election. *Libraries & the Cultural Record, 43*, 1–28.

Pruitt, J. (2010). Gay men's book clubs versus Wisconsin's public libraries: Political perceptions in the absence of dialogue. *Library Quarterly, 80*, 121–141.

Pungitore, V. L. (1995). *Innovation and the library: The adoption of new ideas in public libraries*. Westport, CT: Greenwood.

Raber, D. (2007). ACONDA and ANACONDA: Social change, social responsibility, and librarianship. *Library Trends, 55*, 675–697.

Radical Reference. (2013, October 23). *Rad Ref online reference on hiatus*. Available: http://radicalreference.info/

Raphael, D. D. (1967). *Political theory and the rights of man*. London: Macmillan.

Raseroka, D. (2006). Access to information and knowledge. In R. F. Jorgensen (Ed.), *Human rights in the global information society* (pp. 91–106). Cambridge, MA: MIT Press.

Rawls, J. (1971). *A theory of justice*. Cambridge, MA: Harvard University Press.

Raymond, B. (1979). ACONDA and ANACONDA revisited: A retrospective glance at the sounds of fury of the sixties. *Journal of Library History, 14*, 349–362.

Real, B., McDermott, A. J., Bertot, J. C., & Jaeger, P. T. (in press). Digital inclusion and the Affordable Care Act: Public libraries, politics, policy, and enrollment in "Obamacare." *Public Library Quarterly*.

REFORMA. (2006). *Librarian's toolkit for responding effectively to anti-immigrant sentiment*. Available: http://www.reforma.org/content.asp?contentid=67

Richards, N. M. (2013). The perils of social reading. *Georgetown Law Journal, 101*, 689–724.

Richards, P. S. (2001). Cold War librarianship: Soviet and American activities in support of national foreign policy, 1946–1991. *Libraries & the Cultural Record, 36*, 183–203.

Rioux, K. (2010). Metatheory in library and information science education: A nascent social justice approach. *Journal of Education for Library and Information Science, 51*, 9–17.

Robbins, L. S. (1996). *Censorship and the American library: The American Library Association's response to threats to intellectual freedom*. Westport, CT: Greenwood.

Robbins, L. S. (2000). *The dismissal of Miss Ruth Brown: Civil rights, censorship, and the American library*. Norman: University of Oklahoma Press.

Robbins, L. S. (2007). Responses to the resurrection of Miss Ruth Brown: An essay on the reception of a historical case study. *Libraries & the Cultural Record, 42*, 422–437.

Rockefeller, J. D., & Markey, E. J. (2014). *Letter to the Honorable Thomas Wheeler, July 8, 2014.* Available: http://www.rockefeller.senate.gov/public/index.cfm/files/serve?File_id= 8be5e7f4-93b1-4be6-a90c-725fd591fca6&SK=598C8C8FE97F0C8CF2FE5405532336F7

Rogers, E. M. (1995). *Diffusion of innovations* (4th ed.). New York: Free Press.

Rosenau, J. (2003). *Distant proximities: Dynamics beyond globalization.* Princeton, NJ: Princeton University Press.

Roth, L. (2000). Reflections on the colour of the Internet. In S. Hick, E. F. Halpin, & E. Hoskins (Eds.), *Human rights and the Internet* (pp. 174–184). New York: Macmillan.

Rundle, H. (2014). Who are you empowering? *In the Library with the Leadpipe* [Blog]. Available: http://www.inthelibrarywiththeleadpipe.org/2014/who-are-you-empowering/

Samek, T. (2001). *Intellectual freedom and social responsibility in American librarianship, 1967–1974.* Jefferson, NC: McFarland.

Samek, T. (2005). Ethical reflections on 21st century information work: An address for teachers and librarians. *Progressive Librarian, 25,* 43–61.

Samek, T. (2007). *Librarianship and human rights: A twenty-first century guide.* Oxford: Chandos.

Sarno, D. (2010, November 12). Libraries reinvent themselves as they struggle to remain relevant in the digital age. *Los Angeles Times.* Available: http://articles.latimes.com/print/ 2010/nov/12/business/la-fi-libraries-20101112

Sawhney, H. (2003). Universal service expansion: Two perspectives. *Information Society, 19,* 327–332.

Schenck-Hamlin, D., Han, S-H, & Schenck-Hamlin, B. (2014). Library-led forums on broadband—An inquiry into public deliberation. *Library Quarterly, 84,* 278–293.

Scherer, C. W. (1989). The videocassette recorder and information inequity. *Journal of Communication, 39*(3), 94–103.

Schuman, P. G. (Ed.). (1976). *Social responsibility and libraries: A* Library Journal/School Library Journal *selection.* New York: Bowker.

Schwartz, M. (2013, January). The budget balancing act. *Library Journal,* pp. 38–41.

Schwarz, C. D. (2004). Pro se divorce litigants. *Family Court Review, 42*(4), 655–672.

Selby, M. (2013). Freedom's reading: The discovery of two Alabama Freedom Libraries. *Southeastern Librarian, 61*(3), 11–18.

Self-Represented Litigation Network (SRLN). (2008). *Best practices in court-based programs for the self-represented: Concepts, attributes, issues for exploration, examples, contacts and resources.* Available: http://ncsc.contentdm.oclc.org/cdm/ref/collection/accessfair/id/3na28

Sellars, K. (2002). *The rise and rise of human rights.* Stroud, UK: Sutton.

Selwyn, N., Gorard, S., & Furlong, J. (2005). Whose Internet is it anyway? Exploring adults' (non)use of the Internet in everyday life. *European Journal of Communication, 20*(5), 5–25.

"Senior Spaces." (n.d.). *Old Bridge Public Library.* Available: http://www.infolink.org/ seniorspaces/about.htm

Sennett, R. (1974). *The fall of public man.* New York: Norton.

Sensoy, O., & DiAngelo, R. (2012). *Is everyone really equal? An introduction to key concepts in social justice education.* New York: Teachers College.

Servon, L. (2002). *Bridging the digital divide: Technology, community and public policy.* London: Blackwell.

Shaffer, C. A. (2014). The PATRIOT Act a decade later: A literature review of librarian responses and strategies. *Indiana Libraries, 33*(1), 22–25.

Shavit, D. (1986). *The politics of public librarianship.* Westport, CT: Greenwood.

Shepard, R. T. (2010). The self-represented litigant: Implications for the bench and bar. *Family Court Review, 48*(4), 607–618.

Shera, J. H. (1933). Recent social trends and future library policy. *Library Quarterly, 3,* 339–353.

Shera, J. H. (1949). *Foundations of the public library: Origins of the public library movement in New England, 1629–1855.* Chicago: University of Chicago press.

Shoham, S. (1984). *Organizational adaptation by public libraries.* Westport, CT: Greenwood.

Shuler, J. A., Jaeger, P. T., & Bertot, J. C. (2010). Implications of harmonizing e-government principles and the Federal Depository Library Program (FDLP). *Government Information Quarterly, 27*, 9–16.

Siegler, M. G. (2013, October 13). The end of the library. *TechCrunch* [Blog]. Available: http://techcrunch.com/2013/10/13/the-end-of-the-library/

Sigler, K. I., Jaeger, P. T., Bertot, J. C., DeCoster, E. J., McDermott, A. J., & Langa, L. A. (2012). Public libraries, the Internet, and economic uncertainty. In A. Woodsworth (Ed.), *Advances in librarianship, vol. 34: Librarianship in times of crisis* (pp. 19–35). London: Emerald.

Simpson, I. (2014, July 14). U.S. libraries become front line in fight against homelessness. *Reuters*. Available: http://www.reuters.com/article/2014/07/17/us-usa-homelessness-libraries-idUSKBN0FM16V20140717

Sims, L. (2004). Academic law library web sites. *Legal Reference Services Quarterly, 23*(4), 1–28.

Smith, A. (2014). *Older adults and technology use.* Washington, DC: Pew Research Center. Available: http://www.pewinternet.org/2014/04/03/older-adults-and-technology-use/

Smith, C. E. (1987). Examining the boundaries of *Bounds*: Prison law libraries and access to the courts. *Howard Law Journal, 30*, 27–44.

Smith, E. (1995). Equal information access and the evolution of American democracy. *Journal of Educational Media and Library Sciences, 33*(2), 158–171.

Smith, E. S. (2010). May it please the court: Law students and legal research instruction in prison law libraries, *Legal Reference Services Quarterly, 29*(4), 276–317.

Snukals, B. W., & Sturtevant, G. H., Jr. (2007). Pro se litigation: Best practices from a judge's perspective. *University of Richmond Law Review, 42*, 93–105.

Spieler, E. A. (2013). The paradox of access to civil justice: The "glut" of new lawyers and the persistence of unmet need. *University of Toledo Law Review, 44*, 101–139.

Stanley, L. D. (2003). Beyond access: Psychosocial barriers to computer literacy. *Information Society, 19*, 407–416.

Staudt, R. W., & Hannaford, P. L. (2002). Access to justice for the self-represented litigant: An interdisciplinary investigation by designers and lawyers. *Syracuse Law Review, 52*, 1017–1047.

Steinhardt, R. (1999). The internationalization of domestic law. In R. Steinhardt & A. D'Amato (Eds.), *The Alien Tort Claims Act: An analytical anthology.* Ardsley, NY: Transnational.

Stevenson, S. (2009). Digital divide: A discursive move away from the real inequities. *Information Society, 25*, 1–22.

Stewart, C. (2013, September 11). Income gap between rich and poor is biggest in a century. *Los Angeles Times*. Available: http://articles.latimes.com/2013/sep/11/nation/la-na-nn-income-inequality-20130910

Stielow, F. (2001). Reconsidering "arsenals of a democratic culture": Balancing symbol and practice. In N. Kranich (Ed.), *Libraries and democracy: The cornerstones of liberty* (pp. 3–14). Chicago: American Library Association.

Stinnett, G. (2009). Archival landscape: Archives and human rights. *Progressive Librarian, 32*, 10–20.

Stoffle, C. J., & Tarin, P. A. (1994, July). No place for neutrality: The case for multiculturalism. *Library Journal*, pp. 46–49.

Stone, C. W. (1953). Adult education and the public library. *Library Trends, 1*(4), 437–453.

Streitfeld, D. (2010, September 27). Anger as a private company takes over libraries. *New York Times*. Available: http://www.nytimes.com/2010/09/27/business/27libraries.html?pagewanted=all&_r=0

Strover, S. (2003). Remapping the digital divide. *Information Society, 19*, 275–277.

Sturges, P., & Gastinger, A. (2010). Information literacy as a human right. *Libri, 60*, 195–202.

Suarez, D. (2007). Education professionals and the construction of human rights education. *Comparative Education Review, 51*(1), 48–70.

Subramaniam, M., & Jaeger, P. T. (2010). Modeling inclusive practice? Attracting diverse faculty and future faculty to the information workforce. *Library Trends, 59*(1–2), 109–127.

Subramaniam, M., & Jaeger, P. T. (2011). Weaving diversity into LIS: An examination of diversity course offerings in iSchool programs. *Education for Information, 28*(1), 1–19.

Subramaniam, M., Oxley, R., & Kodama, C. (2013). School librarians as ambassadors of inclusive information access for students with disabilities. *School Library Research, 16*. Available: http://www.ala.org/aasl/sites/ala.org.aasl/files/content/aaslpubsandjournals/slr/vol16/SLR_SchoolLibrariansasAmbassadorsofInclusiveInformationAccess_V16.pdf

Subramaniam, M., Rodriguez-Mori, H., Jaeger, P. T., & Franklin Hill, R. (2012). Diversity-related research in library and information science (LIS): The implications of a decade of diversity doctorates (2000–2009) for supporting inclusive library practices. *Library Quarterly, 82,* 361–377.

Sunstein, C. R. (2004). We need to reclaim the Second Bill of Rights. *Chronicle of Higher Education, 50*(40). Available: http://chronicle.com/weekly/v50/i40/40b00901.htm

Svendsen, G. L. H. (2013). Public libraries as breeding grounds for bonding, bridging and institutional social capital. *Sociologia Ruralis, 53,* 52–73.

Svenonius, E. (2000). *The intellectual foundation of information organization.* Cambridge, MA: MIT Press.

Swank, D. A. (2004). The pro se phenomenon. *BYU Journal of Public Law, 19,* 373–386.

Swigger, B. K. (2012). *The MLS project: An assessment after sixty years.* Lanham, MD: Scarecrow.

Tanner, A., Owens, O. L., Sisson, D., Kornegay, V., Bergeron, C. D., Friedman, D. B., Weis, M., Patterson, L., & Windham, T. (in press). Dodging the debate and dealing with the facts: Using research and the public library to promote understanding of the Affordable Care Act. *Library Quarterly.*

Taylor, J., & Loeb, Z. (2014). Librarian is my occupation: A history of the People's Library of Occupy Wall Street. In M. Morrone (Ed.), *Informed Agitation: Library and Information Skills in Social Justice Movements and Beyond* (pp. 271–288). Sacramento, CA: Library Juice.

Taylor, N. G., Gorham, U., Jaeger, P. T., & Bertot, J. C. (2014). IT and collaborative community services: The roles of the public library, local government, and nonprofit entity partnerships. *International Journal of Public Administration in the Digital Age, 1*(1), 91–107.

Taylor, N. G., Jaeger, P. T., Gorham, U., Bertot, J. C., Lincoln, R., & Larson, E. (2014). The circular continuum of agencies, public libraries, and users: A model of e-government in practice. *Government Information Quarterly, 31,* S1, S18–S25.

Taylor, N. G., Jaeger, P. T., McDermott, A. J., Kodama, C. M., & Bertot, J. C. (2012). Public libraries in the new economy: 21st century skills, the Internet, and community needs. *Public Library Quarterly, 31*(3), 191–219.

Taylor, N. G., Subramaniam, M., & Waugh, A. (2015). The school librarian as learning alchemist: Transforming the future of education. *American Libraries, 46*(3/4), 38–39.

Taylor, R. S. (1962, fall). The process of asking questions. *American Documentation,* pp. 391–396.

Thatcher, M. (1987). Interview for *Women's Own*. Transcript archived at the Margaret Thatcher Foundation: http://www.margaretthatcher.org/document/106689

Thompson, K. M. (2008). The U.S. information infrastructure and libraries: A case study in democracy. *Library Review, 57*(2), 96–106.

Thompson, K. M., & Afzal, W. (2011). A look at information access through physical, intellectual, socio-cultural lenses. *OMNES: The Journal of Multicultural Society , 2*(2), 22–42.

Thompson, K. M., Jaeger, P. T., Taylor, N. G., Subramaniam, M., & Bertot, J. C. (2014). *Digital literacy and digital inclusion: Information policy and the public library.* Lanham, MD: Rowman & Littlefield.

Tomuschat, C. (2003). *Human rights: Between idealism and realism.* Oxford: Oxford University Press.

Trammell, R. S. (1997, September). *Lewis v. Casey* redefines rights previously found in *Bounds v. Smith*—seriously undermining prison law libraries and the ability of inmates to seek justice. *AALL Spectrum,* pp. 10–11.

Travis, H. (2006). Building universal digital libraries: An agenda for copyright reform. *Pepperdine Law Review, 33,* 761–833.

Turner, W. B. (1979). When prisoners sue: A study of prisoner Section 1983 suits in the federal courts. *Harvard Law Review, 92*, 610–663.

Tyler, T. R., Boeckmann, R. J., Smith, H. J., & Huo, Y. J. (1997). *Social justice in a diverse society*. Boulder, CO: Westview.

United Nations. (2011). *International Covenant on Civil and Political Rights, General comment No. 34*. Available: http://www2.ohchr.org/english/bodies/hrc/docs/GC34.pdf

United Nations Educational, Scientific and Cultural Organization, International Federation of Library Associations and Institutions, and National Forum on Information Literacy. (2006). *Beacons of the information society: The Alexandria Proclamation on information literacy and lifelong learning*. Available: http://portal.unesco.org

University of California, Los Angeles. (2003). *UCLA Internet report: Surveying the digital future*. Los Angeles: Anderson Graduate School of Management. Available: http://images. forbes.com/fdc/mediaresourcecenter/UCLA03.pdf

Urban Libraries Council (ULC). (2010). *Partners for the future: Public libraries and local governments creating sustainable communities*. Chicago: Author.

Urban Libraries Council (ULC). (2012). Center for civic engagement (CCE), Hartford public library (HPL). *2012 Innovations—Civic & Community Engagement*. Available: http://www. urbanlibraries.org/center-for-civic-engagement--cce---hartford-public-library--hpl-- innovation-95.php?page_id=48

Urban Libraries Council (ULC). (2013). *2013 top innovators*. Available: http://www. urbanlibraries.org/filebin/pdfs/2013_Top_Innovators_Brochure_Full.pdf

van Dijk, J., & Hacker, K. (2003). The digital divide as a complex and dynamic phenomenon. *Information Society, 19*(4), 315–326.

Van Wormer, N. I. (2007). Help at your fingertips: A twenty-first century response to the pro se phenomenon. *Vanderbilt Law Review, 60*(3), 983–1019.

Varheim, A. (2010). Gracious space: Library programming strategies towards immigrants as tools in the creation of social capital. *Library & Information Science Research, 33*, 12–18.

Ver Eecke, W. (1998). The concept of a "merit good": The ethical dimensions. *Journal of Socio-Economics, 27*(1), 133–153.

Ver Eecke, W. (1999). Public goods: An ideal concept. *Journal of Socio-Economics, 28*(2), 139–156.

Verizon v. FCC, 740 F.3d 623 (D.C. Cir. 2014).

Vlastos, G. (1962). Justice and equality. In R. B. Brandt (Ed.), *Social justice* (pp. 31–72). Englewood Cliffs, NJ: Prentice Hall.

Wan, W. (2014, October 14). Reports of new ban on books in China. *Washington Post*, p. A8.

Waples, D., Carnovsky, L., & Randall, W. M. (1932). The public library in the Depression. *Library Quarterly, 2*, 321–343.

Warren, G. (2004). Reaching out to self-represented litigants through virtual reference and education. In National Center for State Courts, *Future Trends in State Courts 2004* (pp. 95–96). Available: http://ncsc.contentdm.oclc.org/cdm/ref/collection/accessfair/id/138

Warschauer, M. (2003). *Technology and social inclusion: Rethinking the digital divide*. Cambridge, MA: MIT Press.

Werner, O. J. (1970). Law library service to prisoners—The responsibility of nonprison libraries. *Law Library Journal, 63*, 231–240.

Westbrook, L. (2015). "I'm not a social worker"—An information service model for working with patrons in crisis. *Library Quarterly, 85*, 6–25.

Whelan, D. J. (2010). *Indivisible human rights: A history*. Philadelphia: University of Pennsylvania Press.

Whelan, D. L. (2009). SLJ Self-Censorship Survey. *School Library Journal*. Available: http:// www.slj.com/2009/02/collection-development/slj-self-censorship-survey/

White House. (2009). *Vice President Biden launches initiative to bring broadband, jobs to more Americans*. Available: http://www.whitehouse.gov/the_press_office/Vice-President-Biden-Launches-Initiative-to-Bring-Broadband-Jobs-to-More-Americans

Wiegand, W. A. (1986). *The politics of an emerging profession: The American Library Association, 1876–1917*. New York: Greenwood.

Wiegand, W. A. (1989). *An active instrument for propaganda: The American public library during World War I.* Westport, CT: Greenwood.

Wiegand, W. A. (1999). Tunnel vision and blind spots: What the past tells us about the present; Reflections on the twentieth-century history of American librarianship. *Library Quarterly, 69*(1), 1–32.

Wiegand, W. A. (2011). *Main Street Public Library: Community places and reading spaces in the rural heartland, 1876–1956.* Iowa City: University of Iowa Press.

Wikipedia. (2014). Librarianship and human rights in the United States. Available: http://en.wikipedia.org/wiki/Librarianship_and_human_rights_in_the_United_States

Willingham, T. L. (2008). Libraries as civic agents. *Public Library Quarterly, 27*(2), 97–110.

Wilson, K., & Birdi, B. (2008). *The right "man" for the job? The role of empathy in community librarianship.* A research project. Sheffield, UK: University of Sheffield Department of Information Studies.

Wolin, S. S. (1981). The new public philosophy. *Democracy, 1*(4), 23–36.

Wolin, S. S. (1993). Democracy, difference, and re-cognition. *Political Theory, 21,* 464–483.

Wooden, R. A. (2006). The future of public libraries in an Internet age. *National Civic Review, 95*(4), 3–7.

Woodiwiss, A. (2005). *Human rights.* New York: Routledge.

Wresch, W. (1996). *Disconnected: Haves and have-nots in the information age.* New Brunswick, NJ: Rutgers University Press.

Wronka, J. (1998). *Human rights and social policy in the 21st century.* Lanham, MD: University Press of America.

Yaniv, O. (2005, October 19). Immigrants warned on green card cons. *New York Daily News.* Available: http://articles.nydailynews.com/2005-10-19/local/18313877_1_immigrants-application-eligible-countries

Young, I. M. (2006). Responsibility and global justice: A social connection model. *Social Philosophy & Policy, 23*(1), 102–130.

Zabriskie, C. (2013, April 30). Libraries in New York City: Why we give a damn and why you should too. *Huffington Post.* Available: http://www.huffingtonpost.com

Zelenika, I., & Pierce, J. M. (2013). The Internet and other ICTs as tools and catalysts for sustainable development innovation for the 21st century. *Information Development, 29*(3), 217–232.

Zickuhr, K. (2013a). Innovative library services "in the wild." *Pew Research Center Libraries in the Digital Age* [Blog]. Available: http://libraries.pewinternet.org/2013/01/29/innovative-library-services-in-the-wild/

Zickuhr, K. (2013b). *Who's not online and why.* Washington, DC: Pew Research Center. Available: http://www.pewinternet.org/2013/09/25/whos-not-online-and-why/

Zickuhr, K., & Rainie, L. (2014). A new way of looking at public library engagement in America. *American Libraries.* Available: http://americanlibrariesmagazine.org

Zickuhr, K., Rainie, L., & Purcell, K. (2013). *Library services in the digital age.* Washington, DC: Pew Research Center. Available: http://libraries.pewinternet.org/2013/01/22/library-services/

Zorza, R. (2009). An overview of self-represented litigation innovation, its impact, and an approach for the future: An invitation to dialogue. *Family Law Quarterly, 43*(3), 519–542.

Zorza, R. (2010). Public libraries and access to justice. In National Center for State Courts, *Future Trends in State Courts 2006* (pp. 126–129). Available: http://cdm16501.contentdm.oclc.org/cdm/ref/collection/accessfair/id/227

Zorza, R. (2012). The access to justice "sorting hat": Towards a system of triage and intake that maximizes access and outcomes. *Denver University Law Review, 89,* 859–886.

Zukin, C., & Snyder, R. (1984). Passive learning: When the media environment is the message. *Public Opinion Quarterly, 48*(3), 629–638.

Index

About the Authors

Paul T. Jaeger, PhD, JD, is professor and diversity officer of the College of Information Studies and codirector of the Information Policy and Access Center at the University of Maryland. Dr. Jaeger's research focuses on the ways in which law and public policy shape information behavior, particularly for underserved populations. He is the author of more than 150 journal articles and book chapters. This is his ninth book. His other recent books are *Information Worlds: Social Context, Technology, and Information Behavior in the Age of the Internet* (2010) with Gary Burnett; *Public Libraries and the Internet: Roles, Perspectives, and Implications* (2011) with John Carlo Bertot and Charles R. McClure; *Disability and the Internet: Confronting a Digital Divide* (2012); *Public Libraries, Public Policies, and Political Processes: Serving and Transforming Communities in Times of Economic and Political Constraint* (2014) with Ursula Gorham, John Carlo Bertot, and Lindsay C. Sarin; and *Digital Literacy and Digital Inclusion: Information Policy and the Public Library* (2014) with Kim M. Thompson, Natalie Greene Taylor, Mega Subramaniam, and John Carlo Bertot. His research has been funded by the Institute of Museum & Library Services, the National Science Foundation, the American Library Association, the Smithsonian Institution, and the Bill & Melinda Gates Foundation, among others. Dr. Jaeger is editor of *Library Quarterly*, coeditor of the Advances in Librarianship book series, and associate editor of *Government Information Quarterly*. In 2014, Dr. Jaeger received the *Library Journal*/ALISE Excellence in Teaching Award.

Natalie Greene Taylor is a doctoral candidate at the College of Information Studies at the University of Maryland, where she also received her master of library science, specializing in e-government and school library media. She is a graduate research associate at the Information Policy and Access Center (iPAC) where her research has focused on partnerships between libraries and government agencies and the role of school libraries in improving adolescent health and information literacy. Her research interests also include the role of policy in limiting or promoting youth information access, and her dissertation explores adolescents' experiences with digital government health information. She has published articles in *Library & Information Science Research*, *Public Library Quarterly*, *Information Polity*, and *International Journal of Public Administration in the Digital Age*, among others, and coauthored the book *Digital Literacy and Digital Inclusion: Information Policy and the Public Library*. She is also an associate editor of *Library Quarterly*.

Ursula Gorham earned her PhD from the College of Information Studies at the University of Maryland in 2015 and is a graduate research associate at the Information Policy and Access Center (iPAC). She holds a law degree, as well as graduate degrees in library science and public policy, from the University of Maryland. She is admitted to practice law in Maryland and, prior to beginning the doctoral program, served as a law clerk in Maryland appellate and federal bankruptcy courts. Ursula's work at iPAC has focused on e-government partnerships in public libraries and the role of libraries in public policy and political processes. Her research interests also include the accessibility of legal information and court documents, with an emphasis on self-represented litigants, and her dissertation will explore the use of technology to expand access to justice for low-income individuals in the United States. Her work has been published in *Government Information Quarterly*, *Public Library Quarterly*, *Journal of Open Access to Law*, *Information Polity*, and *International Journal of Public Administration in the Digital Age*. She is an associate editor of *Library Quarterly*.

CPSIA information can be obtained at www.ICGtesting.com
Printed in the USA
BVOW03*0950020615

402486BV00001B/2/P